2

success
through

P•L•A•Y

BOOKS BY D. H. RADLER

SUCCESS THROUGH PLAY
with Newell C. Kephart

AMERICAN TEENAGER
with H. H. Remmers

success
through

P·L·A·Y

HOW TO PREPARE YOUR CHILD FOR
SCHOOL ACHIEVEMENT—AND ENJOY IT

by D. H. Radler with Newell C. Kephart
Executive Director,
Achievement Center for Children

Foreword by Richard J. Apell, O.D.,
Gesell Institute of Child Development

Harper & Row, Publishers

New York and Evanston

149311

contents

foreword

IN THIS brief volume Mr. Radler and Dr. Kephart have addressed themselves primarily to parents, especially those parents of preschool and school-age children who are finding the going difficult in school. The writers are enthusiastic, even elated, as to what can happen to a child as the result of basic visual motor skills training. They have reason to be, as I have seen some of the films made at the Glen Haven Achievement Camp which graphically demonstrate the changes that take place in these youngsters. For all their enthusiasm the authors are wisely cautious lest their audience grasp at these training procedures as a panacea to solve all the ills of all children. They emphasize that this is a basic educational program and not a therapeutic one.

"Readiness" as used in this volume implies preparedness to learn and the results of learning. Preparedness to learn depends strongly upon the basic growth of the individual, his natural propensities and biological characteristics. The basic organism can never be discounted in favor of environmental factors alone. A child may be bright, dull, or average; he may be perfect or he may be damaged. These biological factors act as limits to the upper end of the performance range which may be designated as intelligence.

Since many of the children described within this book and many we see at the Gesell Institute behave more at the lower end of their own intelligence range than at the upper, they are forever behind what is expected at their age. In kindergarten they are ready for nursery school activities, in first grade for kindergarten, in second grade for first grade, etc., always behind, never being ready to assimilate what is being learned by the rest of the group. How can such a child learn to read, to do arithmetic, to write, and to play well with his peers unless someone first goes back and fills in the holes and gaps in early visual motor and language development? Often what we see as school problems are not really problems in themselves but symptoms of a lack of early integration of visual, motor, speech, and language skills. And who is the someone that has to go back and fill in these holes in development? Mother or father or both are the most likely candidates. With the help of the psychologist, educator, physician, and optometrist, singly or collectively, combined with some parental insight and common sense, much can be done to make growing up a real enjoyment.

The described techniques here are not new; many have their beginnings with Dr. Montessori some fifty years ago, and she in turn borrowed from others before her. Whereas Dr. Montessori emphasized the development of all the senses, stress now is being placed upon the dominance of vision as the syncretic process of all the senses. Vision here means, "I understand." Vision as a guiding function in each skill is accented. Vision as it is used in this sense is a learned function, and as a learned function can be trained to a higher degree of perfection. This use of vision should not be confused with visual acuity such as 20/20 or that type of designation which is a skill of contour discrimination. (Some credit in part for this approach must be given to Dr. Getman, the optometrist who worked closely with Dr. Kephart and Miss Simpson at the Glen Haven Achievement Camp.)

Parents who undertake these activities with their youngsters will find them to be a starting point for many other games, for what is written here is but a beginning. As parents what could be more satisfying than to watch our offspring grow and develop to be effective members of society and to know the role that our teaching contributed to this end?

RICHARD J. APELL, Optometrist
Director of Visual Department
Gesell Institute of Child Development
New Haven, Connecticut, July 7, 1959

preface

My first child was born on New Year's Day, 1948. This was about the time when the parlor pastime of comparing one's own children with Dr. Gesell's norms had achieved the status of a national fad. As a graduate student in psychology at the University of Chicago—and a proud young father—I was, of course, infected with the same bug.

It was fortunate for my enjoyment of the game (and for my wife and our first child, Scott) that he was in most respects somewhat ahead of the established norms. This, of course, adds to the game the zest of odds-on competition; it is amazing how much fun one can get from boring one's friends to death by recounting, in great detail, one's child's manifest superiority!

What would we have done, however, if, in one or

many specific areas of development, Scott had been *behind* the norms instead of ahead? Chances are we'd have consulted an expert—a doctor, a psychologist or a psychiatrist. Our question would have been: "What should we do? Scott doesn't perform at the level the books say he should." The expert's answer would have been short and simple: "Wait." This is still the answer many experts are giving to such worried parents.

There is another answer, one you can get if the expert to whom you turn for help is in the vanguard of those who keep up-to-date on current research results and new clinical techniques. You'll find that answer in this book.

When Johnny and Suzie enter the first grade at the age of six, they are expected to bring into the classroom with them a background of experience and achievement, a complement of skills, that make a list a good deal longer than Suzie's braids (in Chapter II, you'll see this list spelled out). For those children who bring with them all the equipment they are assumed to have, first grade work is a valuable learning experience. It provides a firm foundation on which can be built later learning experiences that prepare the child for achievement in our complex, highly technological society.

But for the child who is lacking some, or all, of the skills he is assumed to have, the first grade is nothing short of a tragedy. The child finds it impossible to understand and assimilate the material presented by the school. Since each grade level assumes adequate learning at all previous levels, the child falls farther behind each year. Ultimately, he is faced with a choice between two evils: (1) he can give up and thereby fail completely, (2) he can develop learning patterns which permit him to appear to succeed—and simultaneously preclude real success. Among such "gimmicks" is the use of rote memory in place of reading; the child actually "reads" by remembering all the words that go under the picture.

In our society, the primary responsibility for the education of the preschool child falls on the parents. It is their job to provide the child with the equipment he needs to meet the challenge of the first grade. Is waiting the only way to do this job? (When he was about three, my youngest son, Kip, tried to convince me that this was the case. In answer to some command or other— I've forgotten what—he firmly reminded me: "When he's ready to do it, he will.")

Fortunately we can do more than wait. During the past two decades a great deal of research and clinical experience has proven that the basic skills acquired in the first half-dozen years of life are not entirely the result of maturation. Instead, they can be significantly improved—even supplied, where entirely missing—by learning. We now know that "readiness" is not only preparedness to learn, but also, to a significant extent, the *result* of learning.

Furthermore, readiness skills—say, reading readiness —have been shown lately to be complex clusters of more basic abilities: the ability to locate objects in space, for instance, and the ability to "track" a line of type from left to right. Soon after this research discovery, clinicians were devising new, simple techniques for teaching these basic skills, techniques that can be learned and used by the average parent—techniques that require little in the way of equipment and are, therefore, quite inexpensive.

Perhaps best of all for parents and children alike, these techniques are fun. Designed by clinicians who recognize that the preschool child learns most when he is enjoying himself, they are really a form of play, a game, albeit an eminently constructive and infinitely valuable kind of game.

In this book these games, their rules, the materials they use, the purposes they fulfill, the promise they provide, will be described in simple non-technical words and depicted in clear illustrations. We'll begin by presenting the most common readiness skills your child must have when he enters school. We'll break these readiness skills down into the basic skills of which they are comprised. Finally, we'll present simple, clinically proven techniques for teaching each of these basic skills. None of the techniques demand a great deal in the way of equipment. None are so complicated that they are difficult to learn or to use. None are so elaborate that the child sees them as anything more than just plain fun.

In presenting these techniques we are not advocating that all of them be used with all children. Many youngsters are quite prepared for the first grade by the time they are six years old. Others, because of medical or psychological limitations, may never become prepared to go to school. The vast majority of young children, however—normal, happy, healthy youngsters—could get a great deal more out of their initial school experience, in learning and in pleasure, if their basic skills were better developed. No child should be "pushed" beyond his capacity. On the other hand, it is wasteful to fail to recognize the skills that are virtually lying in wait to be developed, and it deprives the child of much satisfaction. We believe that many of the techniques presented in this book can be used to good effect and with enjoyment with many children. We also believe that even the seriously retarded child has untapped potentials which these techniques can uncover and further. For these reasons, we are presenting them here.

Most important of all, these techniques work—not only with the normal child preparing to enter the first grade, but even, in many cases, with the child whose skills are quite undeveloped, the so-called "backward" or "retarded" child.

For example, to Glen Haven Achievement Camp in Colorado in the summer of 1957 came a sixteen-year-old boy whose behavior was close to that of an infant. He spoke very little; he was poorly co-ordinated and couldn't control his muscles at all; he knew nothing of "social life," not even the simplest children's games. Glen Haven's medical director described the boy as "one of the worst cases of epileptic deterioration I have ever seen." Jack had been born an epileptic. Through the years, the disease had taken a terrific toll of his nervous system. At sixteen, Jack was a big boy—and acted like a baby. In desperation his parents brought him to Glen Haven, their hopes held down by previous experiences. Glen Haven's techniques worked, however, as you can see in this letter from Jack's father, a Midwestern business executive.

It is now three months since Jack, Mrs. R——and I returned from Glen Haven Achievement Camp. It occurred to us that you would like to share in our stocktaking of what has happened since.

Foremost has been the shift in the way Mrs. R—— and I try to help Jack in the management of his affairs. Through the new insights of Glen Haven we have concentrated on Jack's developmental needs as against his remedial problems. We have also acquired a good practical understanding of the kind of family guidance structure that is most helpful to Jack's continued growth.

Jack's behavior has continued the improvement pattern started at Camp. Through almost daily volleyball sessions on our driveway (Jack and I painted the court) Jack has developed quite an agility. He can jump in the air and drive the ball with his hands (either one) to a chosen spot. Beyond this, Jack can now "see" the ball in its flight. At first he could not tell whether corner shots were in or out. Now he knows, and adds "I could tell by the sound of the ball on the grass that it was off the court."

Jack now has some sense of distance and is

able to locate objects with reference to each other and himself. He can recall chess situations as we discuss a game we played the previous evening.

Jack's sense of time is beginning to have numerical significance. He now is much more willing to plan events for tomorrow, or postpone something in which he is particularly interested, knowing that "later" will come. We will play chess at "8 tonight" or we will go shopping on "Thursday."

We feel that Jack sees himself and his world more clearly and is beginning to come to terms with social reality. While he is still unable to grasp the other fellow's point of view, he is able to discuss it. He has had a couple of real breakthroughs in objectivity.

Above all else, we note that Jack is much more tractable. He gets up every morning (Monday through Friday to make a 7 A.M. bus) after I wake him. He showers, dresses and shaves without follow-up. He is now trying to learn to accept and handle authority at home and at school.

Jack has taken to drawing while he watches TV in the evening. Dr. G—— saw some of his things, including a most realistic water color of a bus he did one day.

So we feel that the program suggested for Jack's home situation has been most helpful. It seems to work.

And Jack is a remarkably happy fellow these days.

Perceptual skills—the ability to see and understand the world around one, mentioned in the letter from

Jack's father—are the most basic of all. They are, in fact, the logical starting point for all learning, including the development of reading readiness. Since this is so, and since a book that attempted to deal also with language and concept skills would be a huge and cumbersome volume, the coverage of this book is limited to basic perceptual learning. It is also limited to considerations affecting the preschool child, the child from about two or three years of age to about six or seven years.

Despite the fact that I was at one time a student of psychology, I am no psychologist. For the past ten years, I have been a professional writer, specializing in scientific subjects: physics and engineering, biology and medicine, chemistry, psychology, etc. My collaborator on this book asked me to do the actual writing so that his story—essentially a technical story stemming from scientific research—could be read and understood by the widest possible audience. In this collaboration, he is the scientist and I the writer. We both hope that this team effort, which has proven quite fruitful in the past, will be equally fruitful in the present volume.

My collaborator is Dr. Newell C. Kephart, professor of psychology at Purdue University, executive director of the Achievement Center for Children (sponsored by the U.S. Children's Bureau) in Lafayette, Indiana, and director of the Glen Haven, Colorado, Achievement Camp for Children. Dr. Kephart received his bachelor's and master's degrees at the University of Denver, his Ph.D. at the State University of Iowa. For several years he served as mental hygienist of the Wayne County

Training School. Then he served as research analyst with the U.S. Employment Service and the U.S. Navy Bureau of Personnel. In 1945, he joined the staff of the Department of Psychology at Purdue. Dr. Kephart is the author of more than fifty scientific articles and two university textbooks, and co-author, with the late Alfred A. Strauss, M.D. (until his death in 1957 director of the Cove Schools, Racine, Wisconsin), of Volume II of *Psychopathology and Education of the Brain-injured Child,* published by Grune & Stratton.

For me, it has been a great deal of 'fun—as well as a learning process—to work with Dr. Kephart. The title of the book itself is an indication of my hope that reading and using the book will be valuable fun for you, too.

D. H. RADLER

March, 1958

part one

motor skills and how they work

chapter 1 the promise of perceptual training

THE SLIM, attractive woman was smiling as she stood in the doorway of the fourth grade classroom. You would have had to look at her very closely to see the tears in her eyes.

Inside the room her son, Jim, was reading aloud. He read rapidly but clearly, with only a trace of the monotonous singsong of "those little kids in the third grade."

Jim was an average student in the fourth grade. Slightly taller than most of the boys in the room and possessing perhaps a little more poise, he was older than the rest of the children by one year. There was in his stance and expression none of the sullen withdrawal that had marked him throughout his school career, no visible scar of his previous failure.

3

Remembrance of that failure lay behind the tears in his mother's eyes, just as her happiness for his new-found achievement was responsible for her smile.

Jim had started school with joyous expectancy, amplified by the highly vocal pride his father felt over seeing his first son move toward manhood. True, Jim's sister was already in the fifth grade and doing well, but she was a girl. Jim's joy and his father's pride burst into sad little fragments after a few months, when the rest of the first-graders were chanting, "Go, Sally, go!" from their readers and Jim still could not read a word.

He was put in the "slow group" and given extra attention. Still the letters would not become words for him. At the end of the first grade, Jim had learned so little that his teacher decided he must repeat the grade.

"But why *can't* Jimmy read?" his father asked. "His sister is a good student — she's going into the sixth grade now, and she didn't have any trouble learning to read."

Patiently the teacher explained that some children are ready to read ahead of others; that there is no stigma attached to being a little slower than the rest of the class; that Jim surely would "catch up" when he took his first grade work over again.

But Jim didn't catch up. After repeating the grade, he could read a little—but not nearly as well as he should. He was promoted to the second grade in spite of his apparent retardation in order to keep him with other boys and girls nearly his own size and age.

Jim felt the difference, nonetheless. Combined with his sense of frustration, the distance between him and his classmates rankled. He became surly, bitter, a bully. He couldn't find success in the classroom; well, then, he'd find it in fights with the other, younger children. Most of all, he'd "get even" with his younger sister, who could already read as well as Jim although she wouldn't start school for a year.

Soon Jim became a real behavior problem. Moody, withdrawn, jealous of his sisters, he daydreamed instead of studying, fought instead of playing. His second grade report card carried only *D*'s and *F*'s, and Jim expected to be kept back again. But he was promoted, and the vote of confidence served in some way as a stimulus. He began to study hard; his new teacher's encouragement improved his attitude toward his schoolwork and his classmates. Yet he lagged behind, and at the end of the third grade his *D*'s and *F*'s confirmed his over-all achievement level: second grade.

Then began the round of consultations. Jim's mother took him to a medical clinic, where he was examined from head to toe. Diagnosis: Normal. The optometrist was next—could Jim need glasses despite the school report that his vision was normal? He did not; his vision was 20/20. And then the psychologist, for intelligence and personality tests. But the tests revealed that Jim's IQ was within normal range (93, just a little below average) and that his personality, although less pleasant than it might be, was also quite normal.

The psychologist learned that Jim's parents were in-

5

telligent, loving people who had urged their son to exert himself but had not thereby created real anxiety in Jim. They had recognized, too, the jealousy Jim felt toward his sisters and they had attempted to offset it as much as possible by showing him extra affection.

The only real clue to the secret of Jim's school failure lay in his performance on one section of the intelligence tests: the follow-a-maze portion. The psychologist noticed that when Jim encountered a blind alley on a maze, instead of retracing his steps from that point he invariably went back to the beginning. Then the psychologist remembered that Jim read the same way— when he came upon a word he couldn't understand, he went back to the beginning of the sentence. Perhaps Jim's troubles were visual in spite of his 20/20 visual acuity—maybe he didn't see things the way other people do, even if he saw them just as clearly.

Jim was referred to a psychologist who specializes in perception. He took a series of tests in which he copied squares, rectangles and other forms as the first step in determining just how he did see the world around him. In drawing, Jim used his right hand in some cases, his left in others, although he was predominantly right-handed. He turned the paper several times in order to complete a drawing. He drew everything quite small, moving only his hand and fingers. And he drew shapes that were far from accurate copies of the original. For instance, this he drew as this,

and this

as this:

Then, when Jim was asked to copy this figure,

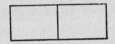

he drew the right half with his right hand, then switched the pencil to his left hand to draw the other half.

Next the psychologist asked Jim to go to the chalkboard and make a dot with his right hand at a point to the left of the mid-line of his body. Then he was asked to draw a line to the right, starting from this point and moving across in front of him. Jim shifted the chalk to his left hand. The psychologist asked him to draw the line with his right hand. Jim put the chalk back in his right hand and moved his body to the left until the dot on the board was to his right instead of his left. The psychologist asked him to go back to his original position and draw the line. Finally, Jim drew the line from left to right, but only after several false starts. He seemed to find it very difficult to use his right hand anywhere except on his right side, or his left hand anywhere except on his left side. The mid-line of his body served, then, as a barrier to his movements.

Next Jim was asked to hold his head still and follow a moving target with his eyes. He did well when both eyes were used, but not at all well with either eye alone. Again the mid-line served as a very real barrier.

Putting a jigsaw puzzle together in another test of form perception, Jim matched each piece to a hole on the basis of its base line only. Thus, he would attempt to put a piece that looked like this:

into a space that looked like this:

It was apparent to the psychologist that again the mid-line was the barrier—Jim made no differentiation between the left and right sides of each puzzle piece.

Finally, the psychologist had Jim read. Jim confused letters *b* and *d*, letters *p* and *q*. He read *saw* as *was*, *dog* as *gob*, *or* as *ro*. In some cases he got each syllable of a longer word right—*yes-ter-day*—but put the syllables together incorrectly in attempting to sound out the word: *teryesday*.

Watching Jim's eyes as he read, the vision specialist saw them move erratically every time Jim encountered an unfamiliar word. And he saw Jim backtrack to the beginning of a sentence every time he ran into trouble —even when he had read the first three or four words correctly.

8

Furthermore, the information that Jim couldn't grasp in print (where the word order is arranged from left to right in *space*) he could understand orally (where the order is arranged not in space but in *time*).

The diagnosis: that Jim never really learned to distinguish between the two sides of his body. This "laterality," which we all take for granted, is a result of learning. Usually it's learned in infancy, when the baby moves his arms or legs, watching them studiously all the while. This seemingly random play is actually a learning process—the child is using it to build up an image of his own body, a visual and kinesthetic awareness of how he fills the space within his own skin. This awareness is basic to motor control; it underlies all the directed movements we later make as older children and adults. It is also fundamental to our perception of the world outside our skins, the left and right or up and down of things, including the differences between letters—*d* is merely *b* flipped over; and between words—*saw* and *was* are identical except for their individual laterality.

This awareness of left and right, then, was the basic skill that Jim had never learned. If it could be taught to him, he should be on his way to success in school. Of course, he would need additional work to co-ordinate eye and hand movements; practice in seeing, first forms, and then words and letters, as they really are; experience in following a target with his eyes until he could scan a line of print easily. But out of this step-by-step process should grow a new perception of things

9

as they are, a new sense of identity with other children, a new feeling of self-confidence—and, of course, a new level of school achievement.

Fortunately for Jim and his family, the school system he attends has on its staff a teacher versed in the techniques of perceptual training. She worked with Jim from December, 1957, to May, 1958, twice a week for a total of twenty hours. At the end of this short period, Jim's school achievement had moved from the second grade to the fourth grade level. He read as well as most of his classmates, better than many. He wrote, easily, words like *arithmetic, everything, neighborhood, telephone, bicycle.* His report card, for the first time, showed *C*'s and one *B* instead of *D*'s and *F*'s. His bullying of smaller children stopped; his jealousy of his sisters decreased; his surly, withdrawn manner was replaced by the normal carefree buoyancy of a ten-year-old.

What fundamental change had inspired this happy blossoming? Just this: Jim learned the difference between right and left. The barrier of his mid-line was gone.

Jim is not an isolated case. Just such a barrier as his stands between many children and happiness and school achievement. For one child, it is the vertical mid-line; for another child, some other equally simple but seemingly insuperable hurdle. All of these handicaps are educational, for they represent a learning process missed or only partially accomplished. As a result, they can be eliminated by educational methods, most of them quite simple, as we shall see later. The important point is this:

Children develop "readinesses" of all kinds by piling one simple skill atop another. Each skill is acquired by a combination of natural maturation on the one hand and learning on the other. Even such a fundamental skill as standing erect and walking is as much learned as it is "natural." In rare cases, children have grown up in the company of animals rather than humans. These "feral" humans, as often as not, walk on all fours instead of on two feet. This is the way they learned to walk—by imitating the four-footed animals around them. Speech, too, is a learned skill; most animals can make noises with their throats, and so can babies, but these noises become words only through learning which sounds produce results and which sounds don't.

Just as we learn to walk and talk, we must learn to see. In the normal human visual mechanism, things are *viewed* accurately—but they are only *understood* as the result of learning. And vision, in the human at least, is as much a matter of understanding as it is of sight. Until the baby learns that a bottle contains milk, he doesn't reach for it. In other words, even though he "sees" the bottle, he fails to see it as a source of satisfying his hunger until experience has enlightened his view.

Because the average child is fairly ready to start school at about the age of six, we tend to view this readiness as inevitable—the result of predetermined development—instead of seeing it as learned. Thus we thrust large numbers of children into the demanding school situation before they are truly prepared for it —before they have learned to meet the demand, in other words.

To restate the central theme of our book:
Readiness for school must be learned.

Because we now know this to be true, we have hope for many children today where yesterday there was only despair. Skills that come from learning can be taught, while those that are innate must "just grow," like Topsy. Although we can do little to accelerate the physical growth of children (and wouldn't want to, in most cases), we can do a great deal about accelerating their intellectual growth (and *do* want to, in many cases). In fact, research has revealed that these methods may provide the very best way to prepare a preschool child for school or to improve the performance of children already in school.

Simple diagnostic methods can reveal perceptual skill deficiencies. They are described in Chapter 3. Simple educational methods can offset these lacks, as they did for Jim. They are outlined in detail in Chapters 4 through 8. These techniques apply not only to the preschool child, but also to the boy or girl who is now in school. They work not only with children of normal intelligence, but also with those whose IQ's are below average, or above. (They have proven valuable also in cases of epilepsy, cerebral palsy, brain damage, etc., but that is a task for the clinician, not the parent or teacher.)

12

What is our evidence for these assertions? It comes from clinical successes such as that with Jim, but it also comes from rigorous scientific research with large numbers of children.

Here is some of that evidence:

Several years ago, psychologists in the Occupational Research Center at Purdue University proved on the basis of more than a million tests that visual skill has a great deal to do with success on the job in industry. The researchers also unearthed the appalling fact that nearly half the industrial population is visually handicapped, and this handicap directly affects efficiency and productivity. (With rare exceptions, industry has done little about this, largely because of the magnitude of the task.)

Early in 1953, Dr. Kephart decided to find out: (1) whether school children have as many visual limitations as industrial workers; and (2) whether here, too, the result is inadequate performance.

In a pilot study, optometrists and psychologists tested the visual skills of 2,200 school children in grades three through twelve. Then they compared the test scores with actual achievement. The findings:

1. About 4 children in every 10 have visual skills below the level required for good schoolwork—just about the same percentage of handicaps as found in industry.

2. A direct relationship exists between visual skill and school performance: children who see well work well, and those who can't see well do poorly.

3. Visual skills can be improved, and this improvement should lead to better school performance and adjustment.

Recently one of Dr. Kephart's former graduate students, Dr. R. G. Lowder, checked on these earlier findings. He studied every child in the first three grades of the Winter Haven, Florida, public schools, 1,510 children in all. On this test, the children were shown seven forms—circle, cross, square, triangle, etc.—and told to "make one just like this."

Each child's copying performance was rated, and the ratings were checked against school achievement. The results:

This test of visual skill is actually more closely related to school achievement than is the standard IQ, or intelligence test.

Educators and psychologists have long sought a way to predict a child's performance in school, but the intelligence test isn't very effective with beginners. Maybe the visual skill test was the "crystal ball" everyone had been looking for . . . .

In co-operation with Dr. Leo Manas of the Illinois College of Optometry and Miss Dorothy Simpson of the Lafayette, Indiana, Public Schools, Dr. Kephart studied the relationship between measures of visual skill and school achievement at the kindergarten level. Some twenty visual skills were tested, including four skills involving motor control of the eyes. As Dr. Kephart put it in his report:

"It is felt that the results of this study demonstrate

14

rather strikingly a substantial relationship between visual skills and school achievement at the kindergarten level.

"Of particular significance is the marked contribution made by the four measures of motor eye movements. *Since at this age these psycho-motor skills are easily trainable, these data suggest that such training would be helpful in increasing achievement among these young children.*" (The italics are mine.)

As we said before, everybody has to learn to see, just as everybody learns to walk and talk. Until visual training was developed, however, all children had to learn the complicated skill of seeing on their own. Nearly half of them learned it so improperly or incompletely that their failure is readily detectable. In addition to these obvious cases, many others with poorly developed visual skills have not come to light—these are often students labeled "stupid," "lazy" or "retarded." This is why tests in schools, offices and factories reveal so many visually handicapped people. Now, with thousands of specialists fully equipped to give visual training (and with hundreds more learning the art) at least the most seriously handicapped children can be helped. And the techniques are so simple that they can often be used by parents and teachers to give normal or slightly handicapped children a welcome helping hand.

In our ever more technical society, education is virtually a prerequisite of success. In terms of school achievement alone, visual training pays off. And, as we saw in the case of Jim, success in school leads to happiness and comfortable relationships with members of the family and with playmates.

And according to another research project, unskilled reading can actually harm a child's eyes.

Working with grade school children from the Lafayette, Indiana, area, Purdue University researchers noticed that as a reading task increases in difficulty, some children move closer and closer to the page. They called in an optometrist, who peered into the children's eyes to see what happened there. (This visual examination, called "retinoscopy," is familiar to everyone who has ever had a vision test. It shows what the focus is doing when the eye is in use. In farsighted people the focus shows a typical "with" movement, and in nearsighted people an "against" movement.)

As these children read, the focus showed increasing "against" movements. Although they had perfectly normal vision, they *acted as if they were nearsighted,* changing their eye focus by 3 diopters—the amount of correction made by a person with blurry 20/250 distance vision. Other children may not show this nearsighted tendency. Instead, they just can't read! Here, lack of visual skill piles up the number of youngsters who can't meet the demands of our increasingly more complex culture. This is where visual training can stop a problem before it gets started. And in Chapter 2, you'll see how vision and intelligence are linked—and how the techniques described in the later chapters can upgrade a child's *intelligence,* as well.

chapter 2 **vision and intelligence**

JIM, the boy we met in Chapter 1, had an IQ of 93 before his perceptual skills were brought up to par. Then his IQ jumped to 106. Is this a fairly typical result or merely an oddity?

Clinical results with individual children and research results with groups of normal as well as retarded children indicate that Jim's case is in no way extraordinary. Just as his IQ was raised, so can you increase the IQ of your own child.

For example, there was the little twelve-year-old girl who would have been completely charming except that she could not control her left eye and often appeared to be cross-eyed. Watching her read or write, you would see her right eye skimming across the page purposefully and rapidly while her left eye wandered aimlessly in all directions. In spite of this lack of what clinicians call "binocular control," this little girl had a better-than-average IQ—her score on the Stanford-Binet was 112. After three months of careful training of her visual skills, however, her IQ on the same test was 124. And, of course, both her appearance and her school performance improved considerably.

Both individual and group results in a research project directed by Dr. Kephart were equally gratifying. In this study twelve children, all of subnormal IQ, were given visual training over a period of eighteen months. *The average increase in IQ for the group was 15 points.* One of the boys included in the study was fourteen years old, with an IQ of 73. He had a twin sister with an IQ of 72 who did not receive this training. At the end of the project both twins were retested. *The girl's IQ was 73; the boy's was 95!*

Another research project has also indicated that normal and high IQ's can be increased by visual training. Dr. and Mrs. C. V. Lyons of San Francisco studied a small group of grade school children, aged seven to eleven. First they gave the children an intelligence test (Primary Mental Abilities). Then for five months each child received intensive visual training. Finally, all the children took the Primary Mental Abilities test again. You would expect the mental age of each child to be about five months higher in any event; this was the average gain of a comparable group of children who did not receive special training. But for the experimental group the gain ranged from a low of five months to a high of *two years,* and *every child but one* in this group gained *more* in mental age than could be expected from "just growing up."

All of these results come as no surprise to psychologists who specialize in perception or to vision specialists accustomed to dealing with the whole child instead of just a pair of eyes. For example, Dr. Arnold Gesell, research consultant of the Gesell Institute of Child Development, wrote several years ago that "vision is the dominant factor in human development," and Dr. Ward C. Halstead, author of *Brain and Intelligence,* put it even more directly when he wrote, "We cannot speak of vision *and* intelligence—they are one and the same thing."

The basis for these statements can readily be seen in the diagram on the next page, printed here by permission.

Fancifully but directly the diagram highlights the fact that "I see" means more than "I look"; it means "I understand." (*Vision, sight, understanding, perception, comprehension*—all these words overlap and blend into one another.) Most of what we learn comes to us through vision, which starts in the eyes, but only when the brain properly interprets and directs our eyes do we really see.

Even before you can look at anything, you must point your eyes in the right direction and focus them for the right distance. Pointing is controlled by twelve voluntary muscles, six for each eye. Focusing is largely involuntary, being controlled directly by the ciliary muscle, an involuntary muscle, and indirectly by the "accommodation-convergence" reflex which keeps a target in focus as it moves toward or away from you.

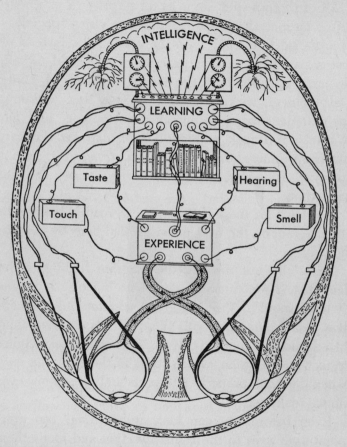

Thus in seeing, complicated voluntary and involuntary muscle-nerve teams must work together rapidly and accurately. They must be exquisitely balanced, precisely timed. Furthermore, as the diagram shows, there is no muscular connection between the two eyes—each operates in its own socket of the skull, separated from its partner by solid bone. Yet these delicately and separately guided moving lenses must work together. Their co-ordinator, of course, is the brain, operating through the central nervous system.

The visual messages received by your eyes have no meaning in and of themselves; they must be related to your own experience, learning and intelligence. Thus to the average person the wiring of a digital computer, or "electronic brain," is chaos in copper. But to the electrical engineer it is a beautifully logical pattern which fits the needs of the machine the way your glove fits your hand. Similarly, this picture looks like a vase.

But after you've been told that it is a drawing of two men glaring at one another, you "see" the profiles there. Then you wonder why you didn't see them before—and soon you see, now the vase, now the faces; the picture has *become* two men in profile as well as a vase. Thus your initial perception was based upon experience with vases; your new perception was based upon the information that there are men's faces in the picture; all subsequent perceptions include *both* experi-

21

ences, so that you now see the faces as often as the vase. (And you'll probably look for faces the next time you see a picture of a vase.)

To you and me such "optical illusions" are simple games; to the beginning reader they are desperately difficult tasks. Just as we see a vase instead of two faces, Johnny or Suzie may see *b* instead of *d* or vice versa. What, then, can the word *bad* mean to them? *Bab? Dab? Dad?* To many children it means all of these things interchangeably: they see the vase as often as the faces. Our job, then, is to teach them to *see;* only then can they *understand*.

Because this fundamental fact is not recognized, our attempts to teach Johnny to read often result in failure. Yet we persist in continuing them, thereby giving numerous children unnecessary experiences of defeat. Our teaching methods usually take the form of word and letter drill, using flash cards and other paraphernalia. Unfortunately, this practice is valueless—it is like attempting to teach someone to play the piano by making him drill Bach fugues before he has ever learned the fundamentals of fingering or even the musical scale! Recently there has been vociferous criticism of the schools because they use "sight" methods (whole words at the outset) instead of "phonics" (starting with letters and their sounds). The truth is that *either* approach is fairly successful with children who are ready to learn to read, but *neither* approach is of any value with the many first-graders who are not ready to read. This is because any approach to reading puts the cart

22

ahead of the horse for children whose "reading problems" are really *lacks of basic perceptual skills.*

These skills are not part of the child's equipment at birth; they must be learned. Unfortunately, the "free play" of the preschool years often fails to provide pertinent learning experiences. Excluding youngsters with physical or emotional handicaps such as brain damage or schizophrenia, the children who have missed these experiences *are the so-called "non-readers," "word-blind" or "retarded" children.*

The process of learning to read begins shortly after birth. It develops in a definite sequence of steps, each a specific skill dependent upon those that came before. It is obvious, for example, that the skill of seeing the difference between *in* and *on* depends on the skill of differentiating between *i* and *o*. In turn, this skill stems from recognizing the separate characteristics of straight and curved lines.

Fortunately for the ease with which children can be trained to see, the abilities that are necessary for adequate vision are simple motor skills that are easily taught and readily learned by below-average as well as average children. Intensive observation of how children develop from birth to school age—most notably the work of Dr. Arnold Gesell and his colleagues in this country and that of the French psychologist, Dr. Jean Piaget—has resulted in a firm understanding of the separate processes which, when put together, become the total personality we see as "a child."

The primary process is *motor development*. This is

the basis upon which is built the child's ability to control his body. Fundamentally the bones of the body —the skeleton—establish the structure of this moving machine; the muscles provide the power; the nervous system is the control network; the brain is the "general manager." In addition to being the result of an order from the brain, each movement made by a developing child is, in itself, an experience which contributes to the basic store of information held by the brain. In other words, movements are not only output; they are *input* as well. What a child does today affects what he will be able to do tomorrow just as directly as the heat of a room controls the behavior of the thermostat on the wall—and through that the future heat of the room. In Chapter 3 we will examine in detail the development of motor skills in the normal child and the relationship of these skills to his growth and achievement. At the moment, let us merely point up the fact that all behavior is movement of one kind or another and that *the movements made by a developing child constitute learning units that contribute to his total store of knowledge.*

Having developed awareness of his own body and having learned to control and integrate its parts, the child then goes on to build up a picture of the world around him. In the beginning, he relates all ideas of form to himself and his own body. For example, the directions he learns first are "toward myself" and "away from myself." Out of this toward-and-away direction sense he later builds ideas of up and down, left and right, etc. It is obvious that this awareness of outside forms is fundamental to reading and indeed to all vision. And here as elsewhere, first things come first—the child must recognize the difference between a straight and a curved line before we can expect him to appreciate the difference between the letter *i* and the letter *o*. In Chapter IV we will trace in detail the development of the idea of form in the normal child.

Having determined the shape and limits of the world within his own skin and having related this learning to the forms in the world around him, the child can move on to an awareness of the vast space outside himself. His first clue comes from the spot in which he is standing—the location of all external objects is related to his own location in space. Again development is from the central nucleus (which is the child himself) outward. The first "space world" develops within arm's reach. Beyond this point all space is essentially visual and demands left-right and up-down orientation, distance judgments and even the visualization of areas that cannot be seen (such as the space immediately *behind* the child). In the latter part of Chapter 4 we will examine in detail this growing appreciation of the space within which the child moves.

The successful completion of the developmental sequence to be covered in Chapters 3 and 4 constitutes the complex entity known as "reading readiness," which we will examine in Chapter 5. Each step in the sequence is *learned* by the child; for this reason, each step can be *taught*, by a parent or a nursery school or kindergarten teacher. The remainder of this book after Chapter 5 presents specific techniques of teaching these steps, one after another. Utilizing these techniques— which are set up as games and are fun—a parent or teacher can make his time investment in education truly effective.

Playing these "games" with children is in itself a "test" of their skills as well. Johnny or Suzie's successes indicate their current level of achievement, just as their failures pinpoint their current needs. Concentrating on *the very next step after the last success* guarantees that the sequence is being developed in order. By this method a parent or teacher can build up perceptual skills naturally and without strain. From these skills comes the complex ability known as "reading readiness."

chapter 3 motor skills —foundation stone of progress

THE VERY first thing that any child does is move. Even before birth the infant is shifting his position, pushing and kicking, a phenomenon that intrigues proud young first-time parents. Immediately after birth he breathes, cries and wriggles—all of which are, of course, muscular movements.

Motor behavior is fundamental for another reason: it is the only behavior that we can directly observe. Thus we can see or hear a man walking, talking, etc., but we have no way of knowing directly whether he is thinking, planning or dreaming. This has led many psychologists, particularly those of the so-called "behaviorist school," to deny that there is *any* behavior in the absence of movement. We do not need to go quite so far, but it is certainly logical to assume that all

27

behavior is basically motor behavior. Thus we find statements such as that by Charles Sherrington in his book, *Man on His Nature,* "As we look along the scale of life . . . muscle is there before nerve and nerve is there before mind. . . . The great collateral branch of life, the plants . . . has never, in any event, developed an animal-like locomotor reaction, nor a muscle, nor a nerve. It has likewise remained without recognizable mind."

There are, of course, many activities in which a human being sits quietly and appears motionless. If you are thinking or planning or worrying or dreaming, you are certainly *behaving,* despite appearances. But psychologists Krech and Crutchfield in *Elements of Psychology,* a recent textbook, tell us that research has revealed a general increase in muscular tension throughout the body during thinking and other "invisible behavior." You have often seen such an increase in tension in yourself and others during heavy thought. It betrays itself in drumming of fingers, tapping of feet, pacing the floor. In addition to this generalized tension, psychologists have discovered localized increases of tension in particular muscle groups. Sensitive electrodes placed over individual muscles and groups of muscles reveal that while you are thinking, you are sending nervous messages. Your muscles contract in response. Suppose, for instance, you recall an insult you have just suffered. If then you think angrily that it would be satisfying to slap the offender, the muscles of your hand and arm will tense as the thought crosses your mind. In some cases this tension is so great that others notice it; in other cases, only enough for you yourself to be aware of this "half-action"; and in some instances, so slight that even *you* don't feel it— but a sensitive electrode can.

Whether covert or overt, motor activity of some kind underlies all behavior, including higher thought processes. In fact, any behavior in which you indulge can function no better than do the basic motor abilities upon which it is based. This chapter will deal with these fundamental skills and their development in the child.

The underlying movement pattern out of which all motor behavior flows is posture. Unfortunately, the charts and diagrams representing "good posture" which we all saw in grade school have created the impression that posture is rigid and stationary. Nothing could be further from the truth. In order to maintain any posture at all—good or bad—we must balance the forces exerted by muscles on one side of the body against those exerted by their opposite numbers. In turn, our nervous systems sense this balance, or lack of it, and hasten to make adjustments so that we maintain a chosen position and don't fall flat on our faces. The zero point of this nerve-muscle balance—the center of the scales, as it were—is the mid-line of the body: one's own center of gravity.

We feel "right" when this mid-line is at right angles to the earth; we're off-balance when the mid-line varies from this perpendicular position. Thus we're comfortable standing up, sitting or lying down in these positions—

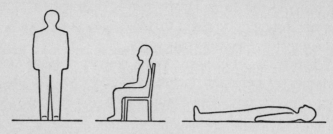

and we're strained in these positions:

One's posture, then, is a dynamic, changing position maintained by muscles and nerves in reaction to the shifting locations of the body's center of gravity.

From this fluid over-all response we derive all our ideas of up and down, right and left, in and out, etc. In other words, directions outside ourselves have meaning to us only in terms of directions within ourselves. For both, the point of reference is the body's center of gravity. It is this point of reference which we lose when we become "dizzy" through illness, injury, over-exertion, overindulgence, etc. Anyone who has ever momentarily lost his zero point for any reason knows that without it the world is a strange and unmanageable place.

30

Success Through Play

Our safety—even our survival—depends upon posture. If we cannot maintain our relationship to the center of gravity (and therefore to the earth itself) we cannot be ready to move quickly and efficiently when danger threatens. For instance, to dodge out of the way of an oncoming automobile, we must know what direction to jump in. The only way we can know this is to know where we are in the first place. Just as we must have a zero point to establish directions in space, we must have a reference point for all movements.

Fortunately, posture is controlled not by the cerebral cortex, the higher brain center which requires conscious thought, but by the cerebellum, the lower brain center which operates constantly and without need of voluntary thought.

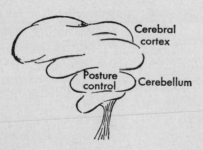

The cerebellum is a mass of brain tissue connecting directly with the spinal cord and the nerve tracts leading to the major muscle groups. In this commanding position between the higher brain and the body's movement system it sits as a censor. When the cerebral cortex works out an elaborate behavior pattern such as that involved in reading or writing, it passes the mes-

31

sage along to the muscles through the cerebellum. If the planned behavior is something you can do without physical harm or major discomfort the cerebellum ratifies the message and permits it to pass. But if the planned behavior would hurt you in any way (such as kicking both feet at once) the cerebellum casts a veto.

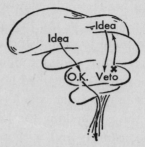

You might think of this veto as a short circuit that returns the behavior patterns to the cerebral cortex to be reworked. By this means nature makes sure that no behavior will result in action that is contrary to the body's structure or to the basic postural mechanisms. Thus we are prevented from injuring ourselves, from losing our orientation and from sacrificing our zero point, to and from which all behavior flows.

Since posture serves as the core of behavior, you want the postural adjustments you can make to be as flexible as possible. If the postural mechanism is stiff and inflexible, the range of action open to you before the cerebellum casts its veto is severely limited. But if your posture is flexible, it permits a wide range of activities. In general, if only a few sets of muscles move to maintain your posture, that posture will be rigid.

But if most of your muscles work together, your posture will be free and easy—and so will all your behavior.

This intimate relationship between posture and behavior was demonstrated clearly in a recent study by Dr. Kephart and graduate student Rudolph Kagerer. They rated the posture of a group of first grade children along a scale ranging from "very rigid" to "very flexible." Then they compared these ratings with the children's school achievement. They found that the children with rigid posture were at the bottom of the class, while those with loose, comfortable posture were at the top.

There was no constitutional difference between the high achievers with flexible posture and the low achievers with rigid posture—they all had good bones, muscles and nerves. The differences lay in how well they had learned to use their bodies. Since this postural flexibility, commonly called "grace," "poise" or "co-ordination," is learned, it can be taught. Many of the techniques described in the later chapters of this book are designed to teach just this skill. Of course we are not concerned with teaching parlor tricks, nor are we attempting to produce a set of bulging muscles. Instead we want to develop the basic grace and ease of movement—co-ordination—that underlies successful performance in *all* areas of behavior.

Co-ordination is essentially composed of two ingredients, known as "laterality" and "directionality." "Laterality" is the inner sense of one's own symmetry: "leftness" and "rightness," or "two-sidedness." We might call it the map of internal space. This map

33

enables the child to operate smoothly with either hand or leg or with both hands or legs. Jim, the boy whose case we described in Chapter 1, was suffering primarily from a failure to develop this sense.

Directionality is the projection into space of laterality—the awareness of left and right (and up and down, before and behind, etc.) in the world around you. We can call this the map of external space. There are, after all, no "real" directions in space; to everyone on earth the sky is "up" and the ground is "down," although people in China are hanging down from the earth when we are standing up on it (and vice versa).

This fancy highlights the often unnoticed fact that space has direction only in relation to the person who is looking at it. Thus directionality is the counterpart in the world *outside* your skin of the sensations you feel *within* your skin—one man's up is another man's down; my left is your right when we are facing each other.

Both maps, the internal and external, depend upon learned postural adjustments and other movement patterns. They are, then, "the knowledge of the muscles." And again, you learn from the inside out. Laterality comes before directionality; the internal map precedes the external.

Our bodies are designed to be excellent right-left detectors. We are bilaterally symmetrical—that is, we have two eyes, two ears, two arms, two legs, etc. Each pair of organs or appendages serves as a sensing device. It sends messages to the brain telling whether a signal comes from the left side or from the right. The nerve systems controlling the left side of the body pass up the spinal cord, cross in the brain stem and enter the right half of the cortex, or higher brain. Similarly, the separate systems for the right side enter the left half of the cortex. Although there is some relationship between the two nerve systems, essentially they are independent of one another. This independence is what makes our bodies such fine left-right detectors.

But even this relatively simple discrimination must be learned. Only by experimenting with the two sides of the body do we come to know which is which. After trying such movements, observing the results, comparing the results with inner sensory impressions, then re-experimenting—only after he has done this a number of times does the child sort out left from right within himself. It is this end product of learning that we call the internal map, or laterality.

There are several stages in the process of learning laterality at which the child can fail and can still make responses which *appear* adequate. Two of these stages

35

are of particular importance. The first is that in which the child learns that as long as he responds equally from both sides he can avoid the problem of distinguishing lateral position. Thus, his movements and his responses will be organized so that both sides of the body are performing the same act at the same time: he will reach for a toy with his right hand, simultaneously making a useless reaching movement with his left. Such a child is avoiding the problem of creating a good internal map by maintaining, as nearly as possible, complete bilateral symmetry. The opposite problem is one in which the child becomes almost completely one-sided. In every activity he performs with one side and merely drags the other side along. Frequently, where he must use both sides of his body, one side will lead and the other side will only follow along without taking an active, constructive part in the performance. In either of these two cases, the child restricts his movement patterns and thereby restricts his learning. He does not gain an adequate appreciation of right and left within himself. Confronted with problems of right and left in external space, he will reflect his difficulty through reversals, inaccuracies and failures; he will read *d* as *b*, *saw* as *was*, etc.

What we have been calling the internal map must be distinguished from "handedness" and from *naming* right and left. Laterality is a feeling of awareness of the two sides of the body and the difference between them. It is probable that for most of us, even after laterality is established, there remains the problem of keeping these relationships straight. Most probably we solve the problem by developing one side as the leading side— we become "right-handed" or "left-handed." (Only a very few people become truly ambidextrous, operating equally well with either hand.) In this connection, it is significant that studies of young children by Gesell and others have shown that "handedness" develops gradually, usually appearing somewhere around the age of two years. Prior to this time the child uses both hands alternately. "Handedness," then, is probably an indication that an internal map has been created, although it can appear in some cases as the result of *inadequate* laterality. Handedness and laterality are linked, but they are not one and the same thing.

In like manner, laterality must be differentiated from *naming* of sides. To ask the child, "Which is your right hand?" is not a test of his laterality. The recognition of the right hand as opposed to the left can be based, after all, on external characteristics of the two parts. Thus, the left hand may be the hand on which you wear a ring, etc. The child's differentiation is then not based on any internal map, but on the observation of superficial characteristics of the external parts themselves.

The development of laterality is extremely important, since it permits us to keep things straight in the world around us. As we have pointed out before, the only difference between a *b* and a *d* is one of laterality. If there is no left and right inside the organism, there can be no projection of this left and right outside the organism; consequently, the differences between *b* and *d* disappear. In this connection psychologist Lotts says, "If we had *only* visual impressions, the words up, down, left, right and so on could have no meaning. One cannot ascribe erectness, inverseness, or slantwise orientation to the universe. 'Upper' in the visual field is what appears nearer the head and could be reached by a tactile member of the head, such as an insect's antenna, if we had one; 'lower' is what appears nearer the feet and could be reached by lower tactile members." Similarly, "left" is to the side we *feel* as left and "right" is to the side we feel as right.

Once the child has developed an internal map and is aware of the right and left sides of his own body, he is ready to build a map of the space outside his body. By experimenting with movement patterns directed toward objects in space, he learns that to reach an object he must make a movement, say, to the right. From this deduction he develops the concept of an object *to the right of himself*. Through a number of such experiences he learns to translate the right-left discrimination *within* himself into a right-left discrimination among objects *outside* himself.

Research workers in the field of child development have consistently noted that appreciation of points in space develops first in relationship to the child himself. Only later do these points develop relationships *between each other*. Thus, early in his development a child locates two objects, each independently, in relation to himself: "That one is to my right; that one is to my left." This has been called "egocentric localization." Later in development the child is able to conceive of one object in relationship to another: "That one is to the right of this one." This later development has been called "objective localization." Piaget, Gesell and others have outlined this developmental sequence: first the child relates each object to *himself;* later he relates objects *to one another.*

One very important factor in the development of directionality is the control of the eyes. Since almost all of our information concerning space and the location of objects in space comes to us through our eyes, it is necessary for us to develop a series of clues by which this visual information can give us the same sense of direction as we formerly received through actually touching something. As young children we do this by comparing *the feeling of where our eyes are pointed* with the physical sensation of touching an object. This is how we learn that when our eyes are pointed in a given direction, this means that the object lies in that direction. In order to learn this lesson well as young children, we must have many experiences in which we make a complicated series of matches between the position of our eyes and the position of our hands in touching objects of all kinds.

The eyes are moved by six voluntary muscles which must be controlled in patterns. The area on which the visual image is projected is quite narrow (about 2 millimeters in diameter). In order to focus the image on this tiny area, the eye must be moved with extreme precision. Given the small "screen" and the six muscles

39

to co-ordinate the eye, learning to focus sharply is very difficult. When the child has learned this control, he matches the movement of his eye to the movement of his hand and thus transfers the directionality information—the external map—from the feeling in his hand and arm to the feeling in his eye. This complex matching procedure requires a great deal of learning to perfect. Only after it has been perfected can the child use his eyes to tell him exactly how far away are the objects that he can't reach with his hand.

One further difficulty is encountered in this matching exercise, and this was the fundamental problem for Jim, whom we met in Chapter 1. When the child is experimenting with basic movement patterns, he refers all movement to the center of his body as the zero point. Thus the young infant in his crib moves both arms at once toward or away from the center of his body. These movement patterns, for the most part, do not overlap. They come to the child as separate directions on each side of the mid-line. If we move a visual target such as a fingertip from left to right, the infant interprets the initial movement as one coming *toward* him. Then, when the target crosses the midline, the movement becomes one going *away* from him. Ultimately, the child must learn that the visual movement is *the same left-to-right movement* even though the direction he felt became switched when the midline was crossed. In other words, the child must learn to reverse his kinesthetic-visual matches every time he crosses the mid-line of his own body. This is the price we pay for being such fine right-left detection devices! And it is a high price for many children, whose problems can be seen in indecision and loss of control when movements cross the mid-line of their bodies.

In later chapters we will describe exercises which will do two things: (1) show how well a child has learned laterality (the internal map) and directionality (the external map); and (2) present valuable learning experiences to provide whatever motor skills may be lacking.

chapter 4 perceptual skills—groundwork for achievement

In MOVIES and on television, the picture blurs when the hero or heroine is knocked unconscious. Anyone who has ever been under ether recognizes this camera technique as a fair representation of how the world looks when its separate elements are so blurred that they don't make sense. The blurriness disappears only as the individual elements of the scene are separated out, identified and integrated into meaningful combinations. Thus, on emerging from a general anesthetic, first you see only a bright mass of shifting patterns, then you sort out one particular moving blur near you, next you pick out enough of its features to recognize it as a human face, and finally you see it as the face of your doctor.

The sort of visual confusion that one faces after unconsciousness of any kind is doubtless quite comparable to the meaningless jumble of sights confronting a newborn baby. Without prior experience as a guide, nothing in the baby's field of vision has any meaning. There is light and dark, motion and stillness, but no meaning—a visual Tower of Babel. Gradually the infant sorts out the motionless background from the moving shapes in front of it. Two things separate these shapes from the background: (1) they move; (2) they hold together—move as a unit. They are, thus, individual moving forms without separate features, without parts and without meaning.

These ill-defined blobs, the infant soon learns, are connected with his own feelings. When one of them increases in size (by coming closer), suddenly food appears in his mouth, certain pleasant sensations from being held and petted appear, and certain unpleasant sensations, including cold and wetness in portions of the anatomy, disappear. Soon the infant learns to identify some characteristic detail of this particular moving blob, the appearance of which predictably leads to making him more comfortable. It is not long before he is able, when he sees this particular characteristic, to *control* the accompanying blob. He discovers that if he makes certain loud noises, the blob can be expected to perform a certain set of actions and all the pleasant sensations will result. Most infants learn to exert this new-found control very quickly, as all parents know.

The infant soon discovers that other blobs do not behave like this one particular blob. They will enter his field of vision, listen to him scream his little lungs out —and nothing happens. By comparing what he sees of the blob that brings comfort and all the other blobs that don't, the very young infant comes to "recognize" Mommy. This process of identifying individual elements in various blobs or masses continues apace. Ultimately the number of recognizable elements becomes so great that it truly characterizes Mommy and does not fit anyone else, even another woman of the same general size and description. To reach this point, the infant goes through a tremendous sequence of individual learning steps. From our vantage point as adults, with a literal billion of such steps already accomplished, it is nearly impossible to conceive of the magnitude of this learning task. You can get some small idea by looking at the room you are in and asking yourself what it is about each item that makes that item recognizable as a chair, a window, a particular man, woman or child with a specific identity, etc. If you put yourself through this questioning process carefully, you will begin to appreciate, to some extent, the tremendous number of details involved in the recognition of any form and how these details must not only be recognized, but must be related one to another. Thus chairs, tables and people all have legs; it is the relationship of these parts to other parts that makes up the recognizable whole.

The fuzzy perception of the newborn is called "globular form" by psychologists. The clear-cut perception of an older child or adult is a new, efficient type of seeing called "integrated form." Globular forms have no real identity because they are not made up of parts. Integrated forms "make sense" because they contain parts which can be identified and relationships between and among these parts which are unique to the form in question. Thus, you or I see a figure made up of four equal sides and four right angles as "a square." We are so familiar with these parts and the relationships among them that we are instantaneously aware of "squareness" as a thing in itself which is familiar and needs no analysis. Without giving it any thought, a square is a square, every bit as much as Gertrude Stein's famous rose is a rose. Think for a moment, however, that there is no squareness in any of the *parts* of the square. There are four lines of equal length which can be put together in infinitely many ways, only one of which forms a square. By the same token, there are four right angles which can comprise any of a host of figures, only one of which is a square. It takes all eight of these elements—and a very definite relationship among them—to create the unique quality of a square.

It is obvious that instantaneous recognition of squareness (or "chairness" or "peopleness") is a much more economical tool of recognition than is the laborious process of sorting out individual parts and figuring out, on the basis of how they are put together, what it is that they comprise. With this economical tool, we have a *quality* which can be used to stand for the total figure and all of its parts. Thus, merely to identify a figure as a square immediately presupposes four equal sides and four right angles put together in a certain way.

As an infant develops his perceptions and moves from globular to integrated form, he faces two major hurdles. The first lies in learning to attend to the details of the mass before him. We see failure to learn this ability reflected in three-, four- and five-year-olds who call any female person "Mommy." Most children leap this earlier hurdle without difficulty. Numbers of them then bog down on the higher-level hurdle—having recognized and differentiated details, they are unable to organize them into an integrated form. This failure to integrate leaves the child with huge collections of elements which must be manipulated one at a time, leading to painfully slow recognition of the forms around him—or to inappropriate or inaccurate recognition.

This failure to integrate is often seen in children who have suffered brain injury of some sort. For example, at Glen Haven Camp one summer, George, a sixteen-year-old boy who had suffered some brain damage as an infant, announced one day that he would attend that night's campfire in disguise. "No one will be able to recognize me," he said. George appeared at the campfire wearing an old felt hat pulled down over his forehead and a red bandana tied around the lower part of his face. All the children recognized him at once, much to his surprise. The next afternoon George announced that he would wear a disguise again that night, and *this* time no one would be able to recognize him. He appeared at the campfire with the same old felt hat pulled down over his forehead, but with a different bandana—a blue one—across the lower part of his face. The rest of the children recognized him, of course, and teased him because he was wearing the very same disguise that he had worn the night before. One of Glen Haven's staff members took George aside to discuss this with him. "Why," he asked, "did you think no one would recognize you when you wore the same hat and bandana you wore last night?" George answered, "Oh, no! I wore a *red* bandana last night and tonight I wore a *blue* one."

George thought that whenever he changed any element in a situation, he thereby changed the total situation. He thought he was disguised the first night because part of his face was covered. When that disguise failed to work, he thought he could make it work merely by changing the color of the bandana around the lower half of his face. This confusion stems from a general inability to deal with all of the elements in a complicated form, such as the human figure, at one time. George deals with them one by one. He therefore sees the entire form as totally changed when any one of its elements is changed.

George's difficulty with disguises is quite similar to the difficulty many children face in learning to read. Before they enter school they have failed to learn the second step in form perception; they remain unable to integrate the elements of a pattern into a meaningful whole. In most of our schools today, children start learning to read by the so-called "look-and-say method." In this method, the over-all shapes of words are pointed out and the child learns to recognize word meanings in terms of these shapes. For example, the word "book" begins with an element that sticks up, has a flat middle section, and then ends with another element that sticks up. Many teachers point this out by outlining the word like this:

By recognizing this over-all pattern

the child reads "book." If he has missed the second step in the development of form perception, however, he remains totally unaware of the individual letters in the word. He still "reads well," however. Every time he sees the familiar pattern he calls out "book" and no one knows that he isn't really reading at all. Soon another word comes along that has the same shape—say, "dark." To the child with inadequate form perception, this word also means "book." Only when his teacher or parent notices that he is reading one word for another which is totally different, does anyone recognize that the child has "a reading problem."

The problem emerges more clearly at a later stage, when teaching switches from "look-and-say" to the "word analysis" method. Here children are asked to break individual words down into their several parts and sound these parts out phonetically. For the average child this step is no harder than the early one, but for the boy or girl whose form perception is inadequate, word analysis is virtually impossible. How is he to break a word down into its parts when, for him, it simply doesn't *have* any parts? Letters do not represent words; they are merely shapes. Syllables are not groups of letters; they are only larger shapes. And words, of course, are merely still larger shapes.

It is usually at this point, when word analysis begins, that "slow readers," "non-readers" and "retarded children" are singled out. In most schools these children are put into special classes or sections where drill—repetitive parroting of letter sounds—is the order of the day. For most of these children the real failure lies, not in inability to associate printed words with spoken words, but instead, in complete failure to associate letters with *anything at all*. For these children, drill is a nightmare of frustration and failure.

Unhappy experiences of this sort can be avoided in advance by assuring that the child develops form perception before he ever starts to learn to read. The simple games described in Chapters 6 through 12 teach this skill. They accomplish this because of the simple fact that form perception develops out of more fundamental motor skills including posture, laterality and directionality. These motor skills can be easily and quickly taught.

49

As we pointed out in an earlier chapter, the ability to recognize and copy a simple form can be measured. So can school achievement. When these two factors were measured by Dr. Lowder in a study of 1,500 first-, second- and third-graders, it became apparent that they are very closely related. In other words, to a great extent we can assure success in school by building in adequate form perception.

Once the ability to recognize forms has developed, the child is ready to move on to the final and most difficult stage of learning to see: the skill known as "space discrimination." Space relationships—distances between objects forward and backward, side to side, etc.—originate in muscle movement. In the beginning, estimates concerning distance are made by feeling the amount of muscular movement necessary to touch an object before us. Sitting up in his playpen, Johnny feels himself making a little muscular effort to touch his nose, not much more to grip the rattle hanging from the rail, but a great deal more to reach the rail itself. Thousands and hundreds of thousands of experiences of this kind soon give Johnny a good rough measure of distance based on the indirect clues which stem from his own muscular activity. The fact that these clues are indirect makes space discrimination a complex learning task. Sound comes to us directly through our ears, brightness and color directly through our eyes, touch directly through our fingertips. Space, on the other hand, is a concept rather than a quality. In the words of psychologists, it is a "second order sensory datum."

For any young child, creating such an intangible concept is difficult. In a very real sense, this business of building up a picture of the space around him is a vicious circle situation: he cannot develop a stable space world until he learns to interpret the information from his senses in terms of a space world. Meanwhile, difficult as this task may be, its importance can scarcely be overestimated. Only through a concept of space can we observe the relationships between things in the world around us. We cannot compare any two objects unless we have an adequate framework of space in which to put them and hold them while we make comparisons. Just as form perception serves to cast the shapes we see into meaningful figures, space perception makes meaningful the relationships between forms.

Many children begin to have their first difficulty in school when they approach the problem of numbers. Quite often their failure is attributed to "being bad in arithmetic," "having no number sense," or "just not trying hard enough." It is quite probable, however, that children who find arithmetic difficult are operating under the handicap of inadequate space discrimination. Mathematics of all kinds deals with groups of objects, such as the number group 1 plus 1; and the characteristics of such groups, such as "the odd numbers 1, 3, 5" and "the even numbers 2, 4, 6." Groups of things can only exist in some space. Obviously the child who has not developed an adequate space world can be expected to have difficulty in dealing with groups such as those basic to all mathematical work.

We have been fond of saying that arithmetic "teaches one to think." This is, of course, an old wives' tale long ago overthrown by psychological research. Arithmetic teaches one to do arithmetic and nothing more. However, the child who has difficulty with space is likely to have trouble with arithmetic and is equally likely to find all thinking difficult. As we have said, we observe the similarities and differences between objects by locating them firmly in space and holding them there with our eyes or with our minds while we observe them. This observation is crucial to all thinking. To group things on the basis of their characteristics, such as separating dogs from cats, and to develop concepts of all kinds, we must observe the similarities and differences between groups of things or events. To pin down the cause for anything that happens, we must observe the effect. Without such observation, all of modern technology, including automobiles and air-conditioners, deepfreezes and jet planes, would be impossible. Even the concept of time is made manageable by translating it into changes in space. For almost all of us, movement in time exists primarily as movement in space—the movement of a hand around the face of a clock!

As we have said, space is measured by the very young child in terms of muscular movements. Soon, however, this process of locating an object by touching it becomes woefully inefficient. The child can reach an arm's length or walk a room's length, but he certainly cannot depend upon movement alone to tell him how far away a moving automobile actually is. Because movement alone is too slow and at any distance too difficult, space measurement is soon turned over to the visual mechanism. Once we have learned to use it, vision can give us rapid estimates of distance in all directions. By the same token, vision can give us numerous estimates all at once; we can quickly look at a number of objects and locate them all in space simultaneously. If we depended on actually touching the objects, we would have to locate each one independently. Even for the average visual situation such as looking at one's surroundings in a small room, locating each object by touch would be an impossible task. This is true, of course, because of the number of individual objects surrounding us at all times, and their distance from us. Of all our senses, vision, the most rapid and the most comprehensive sense, is uniquely fitted to the task of locating all the objects in the world around us.

But even for the simple job of locating one object in space, many different visual adjustments come into play. The one with which most people are most familiar is perspective—the same visual clue that makes a flat painting or photograph appear to have depth. We interpret perspective on the basis of many different clues. If one object overlaps another, we know that it is closer. If lines which appear parallel close to us

53

gradually approach each other in our field of vision, we know that they are moving away, just as parallel railroad tracks appear to meet in the distance.

Obviously, railroad tracks do not meet and most things do not overlap one another. Since we know this to be the case, we use these "impossible situations" as clues to the distance between us and a given object.

Less familiar but equally important is the clue that comes from the location of our own eyes as they change in focus from near to far or vice versa. Each time we shift our gaze in this way, the lenses of our eyes change their shape in order to locate the new object in exactly the same spot on the retina of the eye in which the first object was formerly located. This process is nearly identical to that involved in adjusting a camera lens for the distance of the subject. In the eye, however, the adjustment is automatic and follows immediately upon switching from near to far or from far to near, without requiring conscious effort. The muscles that achieve this wondrous adjustment, the ciliary muscles, do so by relaxing and contracting. Sensitive nerves attached to these muscles feel the degree of contraction or relaxation and pass the information along to the brain; using this information as a clue, the brain makes a further estimate about distance. When considerable contraction is registered, the brain tells us that we are looking at a very close object; when the ciliary muscles are relaxed, we know that we are looking at a very distant object.

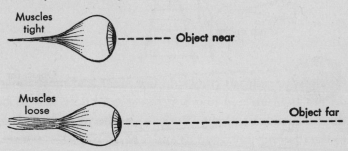

We get further clues about distance from the information the brain receives concerning the direction in which each of our two eyes is looking. Since our eyes are set apart, each one must point a little differently if it is to center on the thing at which we are looking. Thus, any visual target is the apex of a triangle of which the line between the left eye and the right eye is the base. The sides of the triangle are formed by the line of sight of each eye. When we look at a distant object, the apex of the triangle is far removed from the base, making the sides of the triangle nearly parallel. When the object is quite close, the apex will be near the base and the sides of the triangle will form a sharp angle with the base.

In other words, looking at a distance, each of our eyes peers nearly straight ahead, but looking at a near

55

point, they are focused to point in toward each other. The muscles attached to the outside of each eyeball

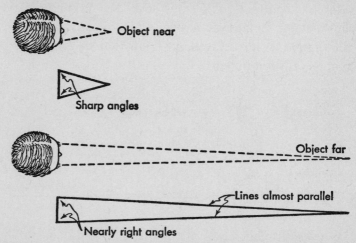

which control these movements relay their degree of contraction or relaxation to the brain. In turn, this information helps tell us how near or how far a given visual object lies. (If you would like to feel this phenomenon taking place, close your eyes and move them around. You will know exactly where they are pointed even though there is no image to guide you. This information comes from the nerves attached to the muscles that move the eyes.)

Further clues about distance come from the size of the image cast upon the retina—the farther away the object lies, the smaller is its size on the eyeball. We know, for instance, that the people on this side of the street are not giants and those on the other side are not pygmies, though they appear quite different in size. What our brains do for us, of course, is to correct *apparent size* into *distance*.

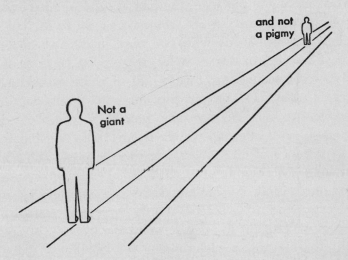

and not a pigmy

Not a giant

We get further information about distance from the location of the image upon each retina. This is the ability that is measured in depth perception tests. We learn a great deal also from the apparent movement of objects as our eyes move. (You can see the former type of phenomenon in an old-fashioned stereopticon or in its more modern counterpart, the 3–D movie. The latter phenomenon you can check the next time you are riding in a car or train. Just watch the telephone poles at a distance from you. They will seem to approach very slowly. As they come closer however, they seem to move faster; the ones right outside your car window fairly whiz by.)

All of these clues concerning the location of the

myriad objects which make up our visual surroundings only serve us if we have learned how to interpret them. The focusing of our eyes, the line of sight of each eye, the apparent size of the objects and so forth, only mean distance to us when we have learned to relate what we feel in our own heads to what there is in the world around us. Finally, all of these individual subtle clues must be put together into a meaningful whole. As you can see, the process is complicated enough even when all we are trying to do is estimate the distance of one object, whether it be standing or moving. The task is even more complex when we attempt to apply it simultaneously to a multiplicity of objects. And it becomes almost incredibly complex when we attempt to keep in mind the location of one object while we are determining the location of many others. This task is what we must do every waking moment of our lives. For example, as you sit in a chair reading this book, you must be aware of your location in the chair, the chair's location in the room, the position of the table next to you, and perhaps of the ash tray and the drinks that are there. If you shift your attention from the book to the door when someone enters, you must remain aware of where the book is, so that you can return to your reading without spending ten minutes looking for the book. From the viewpoint of an adult, it might appear that we are belaboring this point. But think for a moment of how the world looks to a very young child who has just begun to know that a chair is to sit in, a Mommy is to get food and love from, and a rattle is to play with. Each time he shifts his attention from any object to any other, he forgets where the other objects are. Thus, you will often see a young child looking for a rattle all over the room while the rattle is right in his hand, or attempting to sit in a chair two feet away and ending up on the floor, amid loud and surprised bawling. Yet adults know what is behind them without looking and can reach for a favorite pipe or book without turning their heads. Watch a young child sit in a chair and you will appreciate that this awareness of the world he cannot see is much less developed—first he must feel for the chair, then gradually place himself upon it, meanwhile maintaining contact with it with his hands. Often he makes the job easier by facing the chair first, then holding it, then turning around, still with his hand on the chair, and finally sitting down.

The importance of being well oriented in space is equal to the difficulty of the task. In the normal course of operation, reading, writing, adding numbers, or whatever, we deal not with single objects but with the relationships between many different objects. Thus, 2 and 2 equal 4—*if* we can create a mental relationship between the two numbers which matches their numerical meaning on paper. Similarly *g-o* only spells *go* if the proper relationship is maintained between the two letters. If the *o* comes before the *g*, or on top of it, the word is no longer *go*. For the learning process in the early grades of school, a firm grasp of the structure of space is essential, as we have pointed out in this and earlier chapters. This grasp rests almost entirely upon vision. We discover where things are, not only absolutely but in relation to ourselves and to other things outside ourselves, by looking at them. Then we judge their location by reading the signals that are fed from our eyes to our brains. All of these skills must be learned by the young child. Although he can see shortly after he is born, he must undergo a never-ending series of learning experiences in order to put meaning into the visual images cast upon his retina. Because these skills are learned, they can be taught. Most of the remaining chapters of this book will be devoted to outlining simple techniques which can be used by a parent or a teacher to teach the visual skills upon which success in school—and in later life—must be based.

Among the early skills which we can teach the child is crude control of eye movement, each eye alone and then both eyes together. Then we can move on to train the child to match the information he gets from his own changes of eye position with the information he gets from his hand as it moves to touch or to hold objects before him. Ultimately the child must learn to depend entirely upon what he sees, substituting eye movement alone for hand and eye movement together. This is possible only after he experiences enough to match changes in the location, direction, and muscle tension of his eyes with changes previously resulting from movements of all the other parts of his body.

Difficult as all this may sound, it is learned without special effort by perhaps half the children in the world. It is not too great a task, then, to devote a few minutes a day over a period of a few weeks or months to the other half—the children who find learning to read, to write, to add and subtract too difficult—the ones we often call lazy, retarded or stupid. Their failure to learn reflects, in most cases, our failure to teach.

chapter 5 what we expect of the child entering school

To MOST of us the details of how children learn to see presented in the preceding four chapters might seem unnecessarily complicated. After all, children sort of grow, like Topsy, and, in due course, become adults. The process in between may be somewhat painful on occasion, but most children weather it without too much difficulty, don't they? Unfortunately, they do not. As we pointed out in the first chaper, just about every other child has some vision problem beyond that of simple correctable nearsightedness or farsightedness. These problems begin to appear when the child starts kindergarten or first grade. The reason that so many of them appear then is that the "simple tasks" expected of a child entering kindergarten are not nearly as simple as they look.

Success Through Play

The usual kindergarten curriculum demands a certain level of readiness on the part of each child in four areas of behavior—motor, symbolic, social and numerical. Under motor behavior, a kindergarten boy or girl should be able to hop on one foot, skip, broad jump and high jump, throw a ball accurately; draw simple forms such as a circle, a square or a cross; and build with blocks, among other things. Under symbolic behavior, we expect a kindergarten child to be able to tell a connected story recounting some experience he has had, to draw a crude but realistic representation of a scene, to interpret the meaning of a simple picture, to identify missing parts of pictures, and so forth. Under social behavior, a kindergarten boy or girl is expected to dress himself, including lacing his own shoes, to co-operate with other children and to obey necessary commands. Finally, kindergarten children are supposed to be able to count to four, to repeat four digits that are told to them, such as 8–3–9–2, and to know the difference between large and small, big and little, many and few, and similar simple number concepts.

Think about these tasks for a moment and you will recognize in most, if not all of them, an underlying expectation that the child has successfully mastered various major and minor muscle movements and combinations of such movements: that he can control his eye movements; that he can co-ordinate eye and hand motions; that he has developed a true sense of laterality and directionality; that he can perceive a form such

63

as a circle or a square correctly; and even that he can interpret a sequence in space in terms of a sequence in time (more about this later).

The complexity of these "simple tasks" becomes readily apparent after we analyze any one of them in detail. Take, for example, the common task of copying a square. This is such an excellent index of the degree to which a child has developed that it is included at the four-year level on several current intelligence tests. Furthermore, it is an important task, in that the ability to draw a reasonably decent square underlies the later ability to draw a picture or to write letters and numbers.

To begin with, gross motor abilities involving the entire body, and particularly the large muscle groups, are involved in drawing anything. The first and most obvious necessity is the ability to sit up. Equally obvious, the child must be able to hold his head up while he is in a sitting position. He must also be able to move fingers, wrist, hand and arm in a co-ordinated fashion. These movements must be under the child's control and, since drawing a square on paper is a small task, the control must be rather accurate. (It is much easier to make a sweeping large drawing on a blackboard than to draw the same figure in small size on paper.) Furthermore, the child's two arms cannot move together in any symmetrical relation—he must be able to cause the muscles in one arm to respond to one set of commands while those in the other arm act in response to an entirely different pattern of orders.

Each of these gross motor abilities must be learned

as the child develops; he is not born with any of them. Ordinarily, infants learn to hold their heads up and, quite soon after, to maintain themselves in a sitting position. Control of the arms comes later; of the hands, wrists and fingers, still later; and last comes differential control of the two arms working under different movement patterns.

But there is more. In order to draw a square, the child must have learned to co-ordinate his eye movements with his hand movements. As we noted earlier, the recognition of right and left, up and down, forward and backward, and so forth, in space or on paper, develops first within the child's own body in terms of the muscle movements he makes. In order to draw a square he must connect these internal feelings with the visual pattern in front of him so that he knows rapidly and accurately that two of the lines in the square go up and down, while the other two go left and right.

Even more subtle and more difficult is the necessity to begin a movement and then to change the direction of that movement, as one does in getting around the corners of a square. In making this change, the child cannot throw one movement pattern out and start another—he must modulate from one to the other, something like the change of scenes in a movie (known in the trade as a "lap dissolve") in which the first scene has not yet completely faded out before the second scene starts to emerge under it. All of this requires considerable muscle co-ordination. To realize how much, watch any eighteen-month-old baby as he plays.

You will notice that he finds it much easier to start a movement than to stop it. For example, he appears quite poised and well co-ordinated when he begins to run from point A to point B, but as often as not, when he reaches point B and tries to stop, he falls flat on his face.

On top of this difficult co-ordination, in drawing a square the child faces the problem of matching what he does with the pencil to the pattern presented by the square he is copying. In other words, each movement and each change in direction of movement must be controlled by a visual stimulus. This matching process is intricate and subtle. It involves accurate recognition of the form the child is to copy; the translation of this visual recognition into a series of commands sent from the brain to the muscles; translation of the nerve impulses received by the muscles into controlled movement patterns; and, finally, the creation of whole new sets of recognitions, messages and translations based upon the child's own observations of the marks he himself is making in the process of drawing his square. Thus if one of the angles starts to become too wide, the following line must be bent in a little, or if one of the lines ends up too long, the following angle must be sharpened somewhat. (This process of changing one's behavior based on what one has just done, known as "feedback," is essential to all controlled behavior. It underlies the operation of the thermostat in your house —and the amazing performance of the giant "electronic brains.")

Equally complicated is the process the child goes through in translating the square he is to copy—"all of a piece" and existing simultaneously—into the drawing he must make, which he is creating piece by piece over a period of time. This drawing does not really match the original, in the sense of being a simultaneous entity, until it is completed. Thus, when we ask a four- or five-year-old child to copy a square, we are really asking him to make a translation from a simultaneous series of lines *in space* to a non-simultaneous series of lines *in time*. He begins with the original—a total picture in space. In order to reproduce this picture, he must take the parts thereof and put them together as a series in time. This "temporal-spatial translation," as the psychologists call it, is part and parcel of the simplest copying job and, like all other "simple" learned skills, it gives many children a great deal of difficulty.

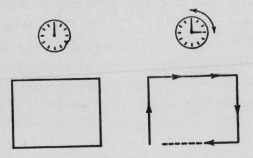

In this one example we can see that even the limited curriculum of the kindergarten demands a great deal of previous basic learning on the part of the child. Until quite recently, this learning had to happen or not happen on a catch-as-catch-can basis; no one could tell a parent or a teacher how to build in the readiness any child needs to begin his school career. Today, both the theory and the practice of readiness training have been worked out in detail. Up to this point, we have dealt primarily with theory. For most of the remainder of this book we will deal with practice. In the several brief chapters that follow, specific techniques for teaching laterality, directionality, dexterity of the arm and shoulder, wrist, hand and finger; eye-hand co-ordination; form perception, space perception, and so forth, will be described. The numerous clinical successes of these techniques when used by Dr. Kephart and many of his colleagues attest to their efficiency and their workability. You will find that if you present them in a spirit of fun the child will accept them as games. Soon you will discover that you are laying a solid groundwork for your child's success in school—and in later life—and both of you will enjoy yourselves in the process.

part two

games for improving
motor skills

chapter 6 angels in
the snow

ALMOST EVERYONE—except people from
the deep South—is familiar with the childhood game of
angels in the snow. In this game the child lies down
in the snow and moves his arms and legs, and then
gets up to look at the patterns created in the snow by
his movements. There are many elements in this simple
game which can be used to aid the child's development.
With very slight modifications it can be used indoors
to make a child aware of the parts of his own body
and to give him practice in muscular control.

The child lies flat on his back on the floor with his
arms at his sides and his feet together. First ask him
to move his feet apart as far as he can, keeping his
knees stiff. Then ask him to move his arms along the
floor until his hands meet above his head, keeping his

71

elbows stiff. Encourage him to press his heels against the floor as he moves his legs, and to press his hands and wrists against the floor as he moves his arms. The feeling of contact with the floor will increase the child's awareness of his hands and feet and their positions at all times during the exercises. Similarly, when the child brings his feet together, encourage him to click his heels, and when he brings his arms back down to his sides, ask him to slap his sides. These physical sensations, plus the sounds he makes and hears, also contribute to awareness of his body and the position that he is in at any moment in time. This awareness is fundamental to body control.

Simple as these movements are, some children may be unable to make them without help. Often we find children who move one arm or one leg without difficulty but cannot seem to move both arms or both legs at the same time. In the beginning you can help such children by moving an arm or leg for them until they get the "feel" of the movement, but as soon as possible have the child complete the movement on his own.

Once the child has learned to make these movements easily and smoothly and equally well on both sides, have him combine the leg and arm movements. Ask him to move his legs apart and at the same time move his arms over his head. Then ask him to bring his legs together and at the same time return his arms to his sides. His heels should click and his hands should slap against his sides at the same time. Thus, the leg and the arm movements must be equally smooth and well co-ordinated and each must take as long as the other. This limits the unconscious trick performed by some children who have difficulty in controlling their muscle movements—namely, to make one movement smoothly and gracefully, and then catch up with a sudden spurt in the other movement.

These combined motions of both legs together, both arms together, or arms and legs at once, are the simplest of all movement patterns. The next step is to have the child move his right leg only, his left leg only, and so on. Often a child will be unable to make these independent movements—when he attempts to move his right leg and keep the left one still, both legs go into action. If this difficulty presents itself, hold down the part that is to be still while the child moves the other limb. The very feel of your hand will make him more aware of the separation between one side and the other and will contribute to his rapidly learning to complete single arm or leg movements without help.

For many children, merely pointing at the right leg and asking them to move it constitutes enough identification so that they can move that leg and not the other. But for other children it may be necessary to touch, rather than point to, the part to be moved. You can hurdle this obstacle rather easily by touching the arm or leg you want moved each time with a constantly lighter pressure until finally you are really only pointing. After one or more such series of repetitions, the child should be responding to the visual stimulus alone.

73

After this single limb control is mastered, go on to have the child move his right leg and right arm together, and then left leg and left arm. If this exercise presents no difficulty, introduce cross-lateral movements—left leg and right arm and vice versa. Finally, the time factor can be changed. Ask the child to move fast, then slow, then in rhythm to your counting, or to music. All of the movements we have discussed can then be repeated with the timing factor added to reinforce the child's awareness of where his limbs are at any given moment in time. Again, this awareness is basic to co-ordinated muscle control.

Now ask the child to turn over on his stomach and repeat all the exercises in this position. Then place a hassock or pillow under his abdomen so that he can be entirely free of the floor, except for a central balance point, merely by raising his shoulders and lifting his legs. This adds an anti-gravity factor which creates greater muscle tension throughout all the muscle systems involved in posturing. This increased tension contributes to body awareness and also to muscle conditioning and control. Remember, however, that this position is quite tiring and the periods of practice should be short, certainly no longer than two or three minutes.

All of these exercises are designed to help the child learn laterality and increase his awareness of his own body. In addition, practice in co-ordinating the timing of the various movements involved builds in bilateral control, in which each side of the child's body maintains its independence but is still integrated with the other side. Finally, practice in timed movements helps the child to see his own activities two ways: (1) as changes in space or position, and (2) as changes in time. This combined view of his own movements is essential to grace and co-ordination. As we have seen in the earlier chapters, these characteristics are the physical underpinning of readiness to learn to see properly, to read, write, draw and so forth.

chapter 7 walking board

SOME OF the simple and yet quite valuable activities of rural childhood are fast disappearing from the American scene as we become a nation of cliff-dwellers. Not too many years ago, virtually every child used to balance himself walking on a railroad track or on top of a wooden fence; most of today's children have missed this experience. This is unfortunate, since balancing on a small surface raised above the ground aids muscular co-ordination and, in a limited area at least, creates a considerable feeling of self-confidence.

A simple walking board can substitute for the railroad track or fence. Get a section of 2 x 4 about 8 feet long and build a bracket for each end that looks like this:

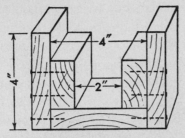

This bracket will permit the board to be set in flat so that the wide surface is up, or on edge so that the narrow surface is up; and will raise the board a few inches off the floor. For beginners or children with any difficulty in balancing, the four-inch surface is used, later the board is turned on edge and the two-inch surface is used.

The first step is to have the child start at one end of the board and walk slowly to the other. If he finds this task in any way difficult you can help him by holding his hand. This help should be withdrawn as soon as possible, but not too suddenly, for some children may become frightened.

It is important that the child walk fairly slowly, since by running across the board he may be able to perform the task without the necessity of balancing himself at all. Each foot should be placed squarely on the board so that both toe and heel make contact at each step.

After the child has learned to walk the board forward, he learns to walk it backward. At this point he will probably need help from the adult. As before, he is encouraged to dispense with this help as soon as possible. He is allowed to look back to see where the

77

next step should be, but is encouraged to learn where the board is behind him without having to look. He will soon find that the task becomes more difficult when he has to look and is easier if he can keep his eyes ahead while walking backward. He may have to explore with his toe before each step to locate the board behind him. He is allowed to do this but is encouraged to learn the direction "straight back" so that such preliminary explorations will no longer be necessary.

The child can now learn to walk the board sidewise. To do this, he stands on the left hand end of the board, with feet together, facing across the board. He then moves his right foot out, shifts his weight and moves his left foot until his feet are together again. This sequence is repeated until he has crossed the board. After each step the feet are brought together again. When he returns from right to left across the board, the sequence of actions is reversed. Again care must be taken to see that he moves slowly and maintains balance at all times.

When he has learned these three basic procedures, the child can be taught to turn on the board. He is asked to walk across the board and, without stepping off, to turn and walk back sidewise. When he has mastered this half turn, he can be asked to walk forward across, turn and return walking forward. The most difficult task is to walk backward across the board, turn and return walking backward. This latter task requires maintaining the difficult backward directionality while turning. Variations and combinations of these routines can be introduced to maintain interest and also to reduce anticipation. Thus the child learns to maintain balance under conditions which cannot be completely foreseen.

Maintaining balance under conditions which are not predictable can be further trained by asking the child to walk to the center of the board, turn and walk back. All combinations of direction and turn can be repeated in the center of the board. Under these conditions, the spring of the board becomes an additional factor which must be considered in maintaining balance. The child should be encouraged to experience this spring and his own resulting sensations. Allow him to "bounce" on the board to discover how it feels to be on a springy surface. Help him if necessary, but encourage him to learn to maintain balance under these unusual conditions.

For children in whom number concepts are beginning to develop, elementary concepts in this area can be combined with balance training. Maximum spring is experienced at the center of the board. When the child is asked to walk out halfway on the board, his springing sensation can reinforce the visual and other clues to "halfway."

The child can be asked to count the steps required to walk across the board, then the steps required to walk halfway across, halfway across and back, etc. Thus he is led to a fuller understanding of these quantitative concepts by the use of his total body in their demonstration.

79

The primary purpose of the walking board is to aid in teaching the child balance and postural responses. Maintaining balance on the board requires an accurate knowledge of right side of the body vs. left side. It develops the laterality that is necessary in such activities as reading, where a left-to-right progression across the line of print must be sustained. As we have noted, it is probable that many reversals of words or letters are due to inadequate laterality.

The board also aids in the development of directionality. Added to the experiences of right and left in maintaining balance are the experiences of forward and backward in progress across the board. Lateral direction is separated from fore-and-aft direction. The former is used in balance, while the latter figures in the goal of the activity. When the spring of the board is added to the activity, the directions up and down are also added.

Spatial orientation and geographical directionality develop in large part from the internal directionality established within the body. Internal directionality is projected into space and becomes the basis for the co-ordinates of external space. Before a stable spatial orientation can be achieved, these internal directionalities must be very thoroughly learned. The walking board can aid in developing spatial orientation and can contribute to these activities, especially arithmetic, where this function has been shown to be important to achievement.

chapter 8 balance board

ANOTHER SIMPLY constructed device to help children learn dynamic body balance is the balance board. This is a square platform 16 x 16 inches in size. Underneath and centrally located is a small post 3 inches high attached to the board by a simple fitted wing nut and bolt. (The bolt head should be countersunk to provide a smooth bottom surface.)

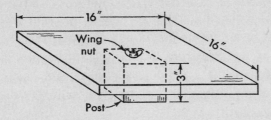

Three sizes of balance posts should be made: 3 x 3,

4 x 4 and 5 x 5 inches. At the beginning, the largest post can be used; as the child develops better balance and more confidence, the smaller posts can be substituted. Some children may have to begin with the board flat on the floor with no post at all until they become accustomed to the task and to the idea of being off the floor.

Start the child with the largest post and, when he can balance without difficulty, change to the middle post. When he can use the middle post with ease, change to the smallest post. If the child has difficulty, pin up a picture or other visual target at his eye level and several feet in front of him. Ask him to keep looking at the picture while balancing on the board. Balancing is easier if the eyes are held still.

When the child has achieved skill in simple balancing, ask him to perform other neuromuscular tasks while balancing on the board. Let him bounce a rubber ball on the floor in front of him and catch it. Begin with a large beach ball and decrease the size until he can use a tennis ball. Let him bounce and catch the ball with both hands, then with the right hand, then with the left.

While balancing on the board ask him to throw objects at a target—beanbag, ringtoss, etc. Suspend a ball by a string from the ceiling so that it swings in front of him like a pendulum about arm's reach away. Ask him to strike out and touch it with his finger as it swings past.

Ask the child to perform simple calisthenics while

balancing on the board. Some children are even able to jump rope on the board. Use the board to help increase awareness of the body and its parts. While balanced on the board ask the child to touch his shoulders, hips, knees, ankles, toes. Cross-identification can be aided by tasks such as, "Touch your left knee with your right hand," etc. Combining maintenance of balance with movements of identification helps to create the body image, the importance of which we detailed earlier.

chapter 9 **drawing games**

ONE OF the most useful, and for the child most enjoyable, training devices is the chalkboard. The board should be large, three feet by four or larger, and should have a plain surface. Decorative designs and ornate frames should be avoided as they are distracting to the child and limit his field of operation.

A suitable board can be made by treating a smooth piece of pressed wood with chalkboard paint which can be obtained from any of the the leading paint manufacturers. Two or three coats of the paint will be required.

When the paint is dry the board should be chalked. This is done by coating the entire surface with chalk, using the flat side of the chalk crayon, and then erasing. This treatment works chalk into the pores of the wood so that lines and heavy chalk marks made later can be completely erased. After each washing, the process of chalking the board should be repeated before the board is used again.

For small children and those with special difficulty, the oversize or kindergarten size chalks should be used. These larger chalks are easier for the small child to grasp and do not require as much manipulative skill as do the standard sizes.

When the board has been prepared, it should be attached to the wall with hinges so that the bottom can swing out. It is important that the child be able to use the board at all possible angles from horizontal to vertical. To the young child "up" means a *vertical* up. When he is asked to translate his actions to paper where up is "toward the top of the sheet," he often finds the transition difficult to make. A hinged chalkboard allows him to experience this directional concept in all its intermediate stages between vertical "up" and horizontal "up." It also gives him the opportunity to experience the difference in gross motor movement when "up" means *above* as opposed to *toward the top*. Again the opportunity to experience the movements in the intermediate positions will facilitate the transition. Such opportunities can easily be provided when the chalkboard is hinged to the wall instead of being fastened rigidly.

Arrange the chalkboard so it can be used in either a standing or a sitting position. A large enough board should be provided so that the full extent of the child's reach, with both arms, is still within the limits of the board space. In this way he can be helped to visualize the results of all possible arm movements by watching the trace he leaves behind on the board as he moves.

The chalkboard provides intensified experience which pencil or crayon and paper cannot supply. The tactual sensations from the rough chalk rubbing over the unglazed surface of the wood act as additional clues in any activity in which the chalkboard is used. Larger activities can be carried out on a chalkboard than are easily possible on paper. The chalkboard can be easily erased so that errors can be corrected or experiments attempted without spoiling the entire product. This ease of alteration gives the child more freedom and produces less stress than do paper and pencil activities. The standing position, which is customary with the chalkboard, is important in many activities. This position can be used with more freedom and more naturalness at the chalkboard and should precede the more rigid and difficult pencil and paper experience.

To use the chalkboard to aid in developing directionality, the adult stands at the board beside the child. He places a dot at random on the board. The child places his chalk on the dot. The adult then plants another dot at random on the board and asks the child to draw from the first to the second dot. The adult then makes another dot and without lifting his chalk from the board, the child draws from the second dot to the third. The game is continued in this manner, the adult always waiting until the child has drawn his line before placing the next dot.

The purpose of this game is to aid the child in establishing and maintaining directionality and changes of direction. For this reason the dots are placed at random and in such a fashion that the child must change the direction of his movement each time.

This technique is somewhat similar to the "connect-the-dot" puzzles commonly encountered, in which the dots are numbered and the child connects them in series. The present method is felt to be superior for training purposes since it can be used with children who have not yet learned to count and also because the presence of too many dots is often distracting to the child.

For children who have difficulty with this activity, use shorter lines and permit the child to pause after drawing each line before he is given the new direction. Some children will have difficulty in establishing the direction in which they should draw and will start off in the wrong direction. Aid the child by calling his attention back to the target dot: call out "here" and tap the dot with the chalk. If necessary, guide the child's hand to help him get started.

Other children will start in the right direction but will be unable to maintain this directionality until they reach the target dot. As a result, their line will wander toward the target. Encourage the child at all times to draw *straight* lines. Shorter distances do not require the child to maintain his directionality for so long a period and hence are easier. If he has trouble, start with short distances and increase their length as the child's skill increases.

Some children can initiate a movement successfully but then have difficulty stopping. Such a problem will result in the child's "overshooting" the target dot. We can aid him by guiding his hand with ours or by providing a cardboard stop at the target dot against which he can bump his chalk. We can give him a stronger stimulus for the stopping response by using larger dots, or by using colored chalk which will produce a dot of a contrasting color to the line he is drawing. We can also help him with the anticipation of his stop by chanting a rhythmic phrase such as "Hit the *dot.*" This phrase should be spoken with distinct rhythm and with a marked accent on the last word. The child can then move in rhythm with the chant and, by following the rhythm, anticipate when he is to stop. Thus he maintains his attention to the problem of stopping during the entire act of drawing the line.

As the child gains skill the adult should place his dots at greater distances and increase the tempo of the game. Be sure, however, that the child comes to a full stop on each dot. At first the child will be distracted if he must cross a line he has already drawn to reach the target dot. When he becomes skillful, however, he can cross and recross previously drawn lines. *Do not attempt to produce a meaningful drawing as an end product of this game.* Use the technique only to aid the child with the problem of changing direction of lines.

Success Through Play

The chalkboard is also useful for beginning drawing activities of children. The child must learn to translate tactual and kinesthetic information, which is his earliest information about the world around him, into visual information. He must also be able to make the opposite translation, from visual to tactual-kinesthetic. These two types of translation must become so efficient and so natural that the two kinds of information become integrated into one.

Learning such translation begins with movement. The child manipulates and investigates objects with his hand while he is looking at them. Thus begins the process of learning. The opposite process is equally important: the child must have opportunity to initiate movements and visually observe their effect. For such learning, an activity is required wherein the movement results in a trace left after the movement has been concluded, which can be observed in relation to the movement just concluded. The chalkboard provides an excellent technique for permitting such observations. By observing the trace on the chalkboard, the child can see as a simultaneous presentation in space what he experienced as a temporal sequence of activities in time. Thus the chalkboard can aid in the temporal-spatial translations which are so important to achievement.

Early activities on the chalkboard should be designed to present to the child a visual counterpart of the movements of his arm and hand. First encourage him to scribble. Random scribbling allows him to initiate movements and then observe the results. Let the child experiment. Encourage him to make large movements, to change direction of movement, to use different patterns of movement and to observe the results.

Children who are having difficulty will find it difficult or impossible to scribble in a free and unrestricted fashion. They make a few short, stabbing strokes with the chalk, using only the fingers or wrist. They cannot make large, flowing movements.

Our first interest is to loosen up the motor approach to the task. Encourage the child to use large, sweeping strokes. You may need to grasp his wrist lightly and guide his hand to achieve freedom of movement. Try to reduce tension and encourage relaxed, free-flowing movement. Music or rhythm may aid the child in developing this freedom. Have him hum or sing while scribbling.

Do not restrict his approach to the task by requiring him to stand at the board in any prescribed position. In these early exercises, allow the chalkboard movements to grow out of the total posturing movements. It is essential that the child learn the transitions from total body adjustments to specific movements of parts. It is also essential that he learn the integration of movement of parts into total posturing adjustments.

Some children encounter difficulty in learning the patterns of neural innervation which will result in a specific movement. The result is a jerky, unco-ordinated lunge. Again we can aid the child by guiding his wrist and by adding to the task response patterns which are more highly co-ordinated, such as vocal patterns. These patterns which he has already learned to smooth out can serve as internal guides to aid him in controlling the more complicated or less well-developed motor patterns demanded by the chalkboard.

When the child has achieved free, fluid movements, we can begin to direct his activity toward the production of meaningful drawings. The easiest form for the child and the first to appear developmentally is the circle. Aim toward a smooth, free movement. Let him experiment first with this circular movement. Later we can encourage him to keep his circles round and to see that they are closed. The closing of the circle is one of the most complicated parts of the task. Closure not only requires accurate guidance of the chalk so that the beginning and end of the line meet, but at the same time involves accurate stopping so there will be no overlap. In addition to its manipulative complexity, closure also requires the beginnings of form perception and awareness of constructing a closed form.

Some children have difficulty in producing a circular motion, particularly in the larger figures. The problem arises when the child is required to cross the mid-line of his body in the course of the movement. Such children have not learned an adequate kinesthetic-visual match. As we said in Chapter 3, initial concepts of direction are built up through tactual and kinesthetic clues. Later these clues must be related to visual data so that the child develops visual direction. The earlier clues are strongly oriented toward the center of the body. When we cross the mid-line, the relation between kinesthetic clues and visual clues must be reversed. Thus if a line is being drawn from left to right, the relationship "toward the right" (visual clue) means "toward the center" (kinesthetic clue). When we cross the mid-line, however, the relationship "toward the right" (visual clue) means "away from the center" (kinesthetic clue).

Children who are having difficulty reversing the relationships at the mid-line of the body will frequently have trouble producing a true circular movement when crossing the mid-line is required. Probably because of this mid-line problem, they will also show difficulty in producing a circle even if the mid-line is not involved. Their circles will be flattened on one side. One half of the movement will appear to be adequate but the other half approximates a straight line.

Such children will need special help with the chalkboard task of drawing a circle. To aid them, draw a large (18-inch diameter) circle on the board with a heavy, wide line. Ask the child to stand in front of the board and a little to the side away from his preferred hand. Then ask him to trace the circle with his finger. If he has difficulty, grasp his wrist lightly and gently guide the hand. Do not force his hand into a circular motion—this will only teach him to be dependent on outside help. Try to guide him only in those portions of the task which he cannot perform and try to insure that he makes an attempt each time before you offer aid. Gradually reduce your aid until he can perform the task guided only by vision and the tactual sensation of his finger rubbing over the board. When this performance is good, ask him to stand before the board and trace the circle in the air just in front of the drawing but without touching the board. When the circular movement has been thus established, ask him to draw a circle on the board with the chalk. We can then move his position toward his preferred hand until the circle is directly in front of him. In this position, he must cross the mid-line of his body in order to complete the circle. Whenever difficulty is encountered, go back to the simplified tasks and work up.

Encourage the child to try all sizes of circles, and to recognize the difference between large and small. Teach him to draw different-size circles upon instruction. Experimental evidence indicates that the preferred method of drawing involves starting at the top and proceeding counter-clockwise. Children who approach the task by this method are more often high achievers in school. Allow the child to experiment with whatever methods he likes. Guide him, however, toward the better methods if possible. Encourage the child to experiment with each hand and if possible guide him toward what appears to be his preferred hand. When performance becomes easy, allow the child to try drawing circles with both hands simultaneously.

When the child has become proficient in drawing the circular form, we can introduce the next exercise. We want the child to be able to reproduce a straight line. Since the vertical line is easier for the child than the horizontal, vertical lines are presented first. Draw a straight vertical line down the chalkboard and ask the child to make one like it. The line should be as long as possible but not so long that the child cannot reach the extremes with ease.

The child will find this task easier if he makes his line in a position slightly off-center toward the dominant hand. The mechanical organization of the bony and muscular structure is such that the movement required by this task is easier if it is slightly off the center of the body. Permit the child to begin in this easier position and move in to the center as he begins to learn. It may be necessary to aid him by guiding his hand until he begins to develop skill.

The task should be performed with the dominant hand and also with the non-dominant hand. The child should also try drawing simultaneous lines with both hands together. Aim for smooth, even performance. This is easier when the line is drawn from top to bottom, since the action of gravity is in the same direction as the movement of the child. After he has become skillful in this task, reverse the direction and ask him to draw from bottom to top, against the pull of gravity. The child should learn the task so that he can perform it without moving his body and while holding his head still.

The next step is the horizontal line. Draw a straight horizontal line on the board and ask the child to make one like it. This task, like the circle, becomes more difficult when the child must cross the mid-line of his body. Therefore begin with relatively short lines which do not cross the mid-line. The child should copy these lines from right to left and also from left to right, with the dominant hand and with the non-dominant hand. Do not force a choice, but where possible guide the child toward a preference for the dominant hand and the left-to-right direction. This direction is preferred because of its constant use in the processes of reading and writing.

When the length of the line is increased, the child may tend to draw an arc instead of a straight line. This difficulty is caused by the mechanics of the arm and shoulder, which makes a slight curve more natural than a truly horizontal movement. The child must learn to modify this natural movement under the guidance of the visual impression. We can aid him by guiding his hand and by presenting heavy horizontal lines and letting him trace over them.

When we ask the child to produce lines which cross the mid-line of his body, he is apt to experience particular difficulty, as explained earlier. He may try to avoid this part of the task by moving his body. He may walk along the board as he draws the line, thus keeping the task always on the same side of his body. Encourage him to complete the task without moving his body. Cut footprints from paper and fasten them to the floor. Ask the child to step on the footprints and complete the line without stepping off the footprints. It is also desirable that he complete his drawing without moving his head or trunk. Gently hold his head if necessary, until he is able to draw the line without head movement.

When he has mastered vertical and horizontal lines, the child has the necessary skills to complete a square. This task involves the additional problem of stopping and changing direction at each corner. The child may indicate his difficulty with this problem by rounding the corners. We can aid him by holding a ruler near the corner to stop his chalk and help him change direction. It may be desirable to use a template, or flat profile outline of a square, cut from cardboard, to help him complete the square. Increasing the strength of the visual stimulus by drawing a heavy square and letting the child trace over it may also aid him.

The most difficult task for the child is that of the diagonal line. This diagonal direction can be introduced by asking the child to copy a triangle. The child who has difficulty with diagonals will indicate his problem by drawing "stair-stepped" lines or wandering off direction in the course of his line. He will have particular trouble at corners in determining the new direction. The result will be "dog-eared" corners. The child may need all of the types of help described above to master the diagonal direction. When he has mastered the triangle, the task can be increased in difficulty by substituting a diamond.

In this discussion, the various figures and movements have been described in the order of their difficulty as though each early skill is completed before the next becomes possible. This segmenting is convenient for the purpose of discussion and makes it easier for us to follow the child's development. There is, however, a great deal of overlap in the child's learning. His processes of development cannot be categorized in practice as they can in theory. Several of the skills we have been discussing will be developing at one time. We must follow the lead of the child in planning his training. Although in general he will follow the course of development described here, there will be many variations in any individual case. Therefore we may be working in several areas of learning at one time. It is best to let the child tell us by his behavior where his difficulties are. Then we can give him special help in these areas. We will be more successful if we follow the developmental process in broad outline but vary our approach within the details as demanded by the individual child and his own development pattern.

chapter 10 **pegboard games**

ANOTHER EFFECTIVE game uses a pegboard —a board in which rows of holes have been drilled. A piece of acoustic ceiling tile will do very well. The holes should be arranged evenly in straight rows and columns. A minimum of 100 holes is required, arranged in ten rows, ten holes to the row. Pegs of various colors which can be fitted into the holes should be procured. Plastic golf tees with half an inch snipped off the sharp end will work quite well with the acoustic tile. Enough pegs of each color to permit building a reasonably sized form are required. It is desirable to use pegs of such a design that when two are placed adjacent in the board the tops of the pegs will be close together. For this reason golf tees are recommended, since in a ceiling tile the heads of the tees almost touch when the pegs are in adjacent holes.

Two boards and two sets of pegs are provided, one for the child and one for the adult. On his board, the adult outlines a simple figure—square, oblong, triangle, etc. This figure is then shown to the child and he is asked to make one like it on his own board. He may look at the form to be copied during the entire time that he is constructing his copy.

This task may prove somewhat difficult for the child. The construction of the figure is broken up into a large number of elements: pegs. He must maintain the form while he deals with these elements one at a time. Thus he is required to hold the form firmly in mind over a relatively long period of time and in the face of distracting activities. In addition, he must build up the form slowly, a piece at a time. It is therefore necessary for him to translate the simultaneous presentation in space which he sees on the adult's board into a temporal series of events: placement of pegs in time. The task is made more difficult by the fact that the manipulative motions necessary to place the pegs slow the process and thus increase the length of the temporal series.

Some children will have difficulty holding the form in mind amid the distraction created by the large number of additional holes. They may start to construct a straight line of pegs and be drawn off into a slanting or angled line. Such difficulties will be especially apparent if the child's concept of directionality for lines is weak. For such a child we may need to provide additional help with the task by cutting out a cardboard template in the shape of the form we are presenting and laying this template on his board as a guide. He can then place pegs in contact with the template and use the resulting tactual and kinesthetic clues to aid him in maintaining the form against the distraction. After his performance improves, we can dispense with the use of the template.

Children whose basic idea of form is weak will find difficulty in maintaining the form during the task. For such children, begin with extremely simple forms, perhaps a row of two pegs only. As the child improves, increase the difficulty until he can copy a straight row of pegs the entire length of the board. When he can produce a straight vertical row and a straight horizontal row, move on to simple closed figures. He may also need a template (a ruler laid along a row of holes) to help him keep his rows straight.

When the child has become adept at constructing simple forms, the difficulty of the task can be increased by increasing the complexity of the forms and by adding color as a part of the task. Different portions of the forms can be outlined with different-colored pegs. Color patterns such as red, green; red, red, green; or red, red, green, green, etc. can be superimposed upon the linear forms.

All of these pegboard games contribute to laterality and directionality, but even more important, they help solidify form perception—a basic factor in reading readiness.

chapter 11 **ball games**

A SIMPLE ball hanging from a string (known as the Marsden ball) can be used in a number of games that contribute to eye control and eye-hand co-ordination.

A soft rubber ball about the size of a tennis ball is suspended by a string from the ceiling or, if the technique is used outdoors, from an overhanging tree limb or similar support. The string can be attached to the ball by driving a small cup hook into the rubber and tying the string to this hook. When the opposite end of the string is attached to the ceiling, the ball swings as a pendulum. It can be swung laterally before the child, in a back-and-forth direction, or with a circular motion around him. By altering the length of the string, the timing of the swing can be slowed or made more rapid. Larger balls may be used initially for younger children or children having particular difficulty. As they become more adept, the size of the ball can be decreased.

The child stands about arm's length from the ball with the pivot line of the string directly in front of him. The adult then pulls the ball to one side and releases it, letting it swing across in front of the child by its own weight. Do not throw or push the ball. Allow it to swing as a free pendulum. The child is instructed to reach out and touch the ball with his finger as it passes in front of him. He must reach out and contact the ball directly in one movement. He is not allowed to thrust his finger into the path of the ball and wait for it to hit his finger. He is given a starting point for his finger each time so that he thrusts out with a definite, prescribed movement. The first starting position will be the shoulder. The child is instructed to hold his hand beside his shoulder with his finger pointed ahead. When the ball passes, he is to thrust out and touch the ball. Other starting positions will be the eyes and the hip.

Always he is to thrust out in one steady movement, not to wander or search for the ball. He is to keep his head still, following the ball with his eyes.

This technique requires the child to follow a moving target and to respond in terms of the position of the target. It requires accurate timing and a synthesis between the visual system and the motor system. It aids the child in developing the vital translation between kinesthetic-tactual data and visual data. He must follow the ball with his eyes as though he were following it with his finger and must learn to obtain the same information through his ocular following as he received earlier through manual following.

Many children will be found to have difficulty in performing this task. For them we may have to start with simplified versions of the task and gradually, as they gain skill, increase its difficulty. Thus the child may need first to learn to reach out and touch the ball while it is standing still. For such a child we would use a preliminary technique in which the ball is not swung but is allowed to hang motionless. Allow the child to position his finger within an inch or two of the ball before he thrusts at it. Then gradually, being sure he masters each stage before proceeding to the next, move the starting position back until he can thrust from his shoulder.

We may need to swing the ball through a very small arc to permit the child to achieve. We can then increase the length of the arc gradually until accurate following and anticipation are mastered. We may need to let him follow with his finger at first so that he can learn to match visual following with manual following. Later we can ask him to begin translating from one to the other by waiting until the ball starts swinging before he begins following it with his finger. He can thus be moved along until he can use visual data alone.

When the child has become adept at the task of hitting the ball, we want to be sure that he is following it continuously and not just depending on a split-second awareness of the ball in a certain position to guide his aim. Certain children will learn how to avoid the demands of the swinging ball task by paying attention only to a small area directly in front of them. When they see the ball in this area, they thrust out. They have not followed the ball but have depended upon speed in a single perception for their performance—something like looking for a single frame in a movie film instead of following the action. If a child has good perceptual speed, he may be able to perform well by this method. We can force him out of this restricted method by varying the procedure. Instruct the child to thrust when you call out, "Now." He does not know when you are going to give the signal and he must thrust immediately when he hears you. Under these conditions he is required to maintain readiness to respond at all times. Only by following the ball can he be ready at any time you may signal. It is well to insert this variation into the training procedure as soon as possible to insure that the proper method is being used.

When the child has mastered the ball as it swings laterally to his body, we can move on to a fore-and-aft direction. In this procedure the adult pulls the ball on a line directly in front of the child and lets it swing. The ball then moves toward and away from the child. The child reaches out with his hand underneath the ball with his finger pointed upward. He then moves his hand up so that his finger touches the ball from underneath. He should start in the prescribed starting position and execute the response in one continuous movement. He should hit the ball squarely from underneath; not position his finger and wait for the ball to swing into it. By paying attention to his thrusts, he can observe the direction and extent of his miss on each trial.

This part of the technique is more difficult, since it requires increased awareness of position of an object in space. There are many clues to space, as we have said before. No one clue is in itself adequate to give us the information necessary for accurate spatial localization. To insure that the child does not come to put too much dependence on one or a limited number of clues, we ask him to thrust upon signal as we did in the earlier lateral swinging procedure.

When the child begins to learn the task with his finger, he may be given a short bat with which to bunt the ball. It is desirable that these ball techniques be learned with the finger first. The tactual stimulation of the finger actually touching the ball, added to the visual stimulation, makes early learning more rapid and more thorough. When the bat is used, the child is encouraged to reach out and meet the ball; not to hold his bat out and let the ball hit it.

This bat or a longer and thinner pointer can be used with the ball swinging laterally to train judgments over a longer distance. Again, have the child experience the tactual stimulation through the finger first because of its value in the learning process.

The process of hunting the ball involves spatial judgment and following a target in the side-to-side and fore-and-aft directions. In addition, timing and rhythm are required, making the technique useful in the training of these factors. Since it is desirable that the movements involved remain dynamically related to the posturing abilities, it is advisable to have the child perform the ball routines while balancing on the balance board. Here the visual following process must remain related to posturing abilities: while following visually, the child must be able to remain posturally oriented and balanced. The child is aided in establishing such visual-postural relationships by performing the task while balanced on the board.

In most children it will be found that, after a visual-motor translation has been learned adequately, additional skill in visual following will be useful. Because of the complexity of ocular movements and the high degree of precision required, ocular-motor skills must be developed to a very high degree if the child is to perform successfully in such highly visual tasks as reading. It should be pointed out, however, that unless ocular skills are thoroughly matched to motor skills, meaningful relationships are avoided and the child learns an isolated, inefficient skill. Therefore, don't present him with the games described below until you are sure that the skills described above have been mastered.

Ocular pursuit movements can be trained with the Marsden ball by asking the child to watch the ball as it swings back and forth. He should be cautioned to hold his head still and follow the ball with his eyes alone, and encouraged not to lose sight of the ball at any time. For older children we may paste cutout letters of the alphabet on the surface of the ball. As it swings the child is asked to find as quickly as he can an *a*, then a *b*, etc. The ball should be seen clearly at all times.

The ball is then swung laterally and in a fore-and-aft direction as before. It can then be swung diagonally— from far left to near right, etc. These diagonal movements are the most difficult to master. They should not be introduced until skill in the lateral movements has been achieved. Later the child is asked to lie on his back on the floor and the ball is swung in a circular movement above him as he follows it with his eyes. During all these procedures the adult watches the child's eyes to insure that the following movements are smooth and accurate. When movements are not smooth, encourage the child to "keep his eye on the ball."

Ocular motor control develops in a single eye first. When each eye singly has been brought under control, binocular control develops. It is important that this developmental sequence be followed in training. The child must learn the translation of the visual data from one eye to kinesthetic data. He must learn the same translation from the other eye. Only then can he put the two eyes together to achieve true binocular performance. Unless there is adequate learning of functions from each eye separately, a pseudo-binocularity develops. In such a case the two eyes perform symmetrically, but do not perform as a team. The performance is stilted and rigid. The information yielded is inefficient and incomplete. The child is not getting the increased data provided by two eyes but is simply using two as though they were one.

For this reason we want to teach the child matching skills first under monocular conditions, then under binocular conditions. Monocular practice can be obtained by covering one eye during the training activities.

Frequently the child who is having difficulty will object to having one eye covered. Since his visual skills are rigid and inefficient, any interference with his procedure requiring a change of method causes him great difficulty. Therefore he objects to such interference. Covering an eye can represent such an interference. Do not force the child to cover an eye. His problem can be met through motivating him to try the new experience. Occluders designed as part of a game—call them "pirate patches"—will accomplish the desired result and at the same time not arouse anxiety or insecurity in the child.

All of the routines discussed above should be performed skillfully with either eye alone and with both eyes together. Be sure that monocular performance is developing adequately before introducing binocular training.

Further training of ocular pursuits can be done with a common lead pencil. Obtain a pencil with an eraser. Drive a thumbtack through the eraser so that the head of the tack is parallel to the length of the pencil. Hold the pencil upright before the child's eyes and about

20 inches before his face. Ask him if he sees the head of the tack. Then say, "Now watch it, wherever it goes." Move the pencil about 18 inches to his right, following an arc of a circle of which the child is the center and with a radius of 20 inches. Next move the pencil laterally to the child's left until it is 18 inches to his left. If the child moves his head instead of moving his eyes, ask him to hold his head still. If he is unable to do so, lightly hold his head with your hand. Repeat the lateral movement of the pencil until he follows with his eyes, holding his head still. Watch closely the movements of his eyes as he follows the pencil. Observe whether the movements are smooth or jerky. Since control of eye movement is an extremely precise task, watch very closely; lack of control may be shown by extremely small spasms. The eyes should move as smoothly as ice cubes in a glass of water. Any jerking or unevenness is an indication of lack of complete control.

Following this lateral motion, go on to fore-and-aft movements, up-and-down movements, and, finally, diagonal motions.

Watch the two eyes working together. Observe whether they maintain their relationship to each other or whether one wanders off from the target. The loss of relationship may be apparent only at the extremes of the movement or may come and go during the movement. Observe whether both eyes are following or whether one eye is leading and the other simply being pulled along. This relationship can usually be observed by watching the timing of the two eyes. Does one get ahead of the other or do they stay together? In some cases one eye will move but not the other.

Observe whether the child is always on target or whether he loses it from time to time. If he loses the target, can he regain it promptly or does he have to "look around" for it? Does he overshoot the target and have to wait for it to catch up?

Pay particular attention to the performance whenever the target crosses the mid-line of the child's body. Many children have trouble in crossing the mid-line and will reveal this fact by a slight jerk in the movement at this point.

After the child has mastered all the ocular pursuits —lateral, fore-and-aft, vertical and diagonal—he has the ability to control his eye movements smoothly and efficiently. This ability is a cornerstone of the complex of skills known as reading readiness.

chapter 12 **a word to parents and teachers**

THE BOY we met in Chapter 1, named Jim, started as a "retarded child" before perceptual training. After this training, however, he became a capable student whose IQ moved from 93 to 106, and—more important—a happy, well-adjusted child.

The training Jim received was in no way different from the simple gamelike techniques we have just described in Chapters 6 through 11. Starting with a less retarded child than Jim and applying these techniques, you will get less dramatic results, of course. The important thing is that with *most* children you will get *some* results which will contribute to their success in school and thereafter.

In order to describe these techniques in an understandable and uncluttered fashion, and to indicate what equipment is needed, our discussion in Chapters 6 through 11 was, of necessity, straightforward and dry, without humor or whimsy. The imaginative parent or nursery school or kindergarten teacher will, of course, supply the light touch in using these techniques. Each one of the exercises is similar or identical to the little games that children play. Each one can carry a fanciful name, such as "angels in the snow," rather than the bare description presented here—"balance board," "walking board," etc. A story of some sort can be woven around each game to make it more enjoyable for the child and to increase his motivation. When he reaches or stretches, have him reach or stretch *for* something—the brass ring on the merry-go-round, for example. When he walks across the walking board, make the balancing technique into a meaningful trip— call the board "London Bridge" or some other span with which the child may be familiar. Each parent or teacher knows best how to have fun with his children. The ideas presented here are not suggestions, but rather examples of the sort of fun that can be introduced into the learning experiences covered in the past few chapters.

Remember also that the techniques described in Chapters 6 through 11 are diagnostic as well as educational. By watching a child perform, one can get a fairly accurate idea of how far along the child is in the development of the visual-motor skills comprising school readiness. The boy or girl who breezes through all of these games without hesitation or miss requires no further training. On the other hand, the child who encounters difficulty with any of them needs continued experience before he is really ready to learn to read, write, add and subtract, and so on.

In no sense are the techniques of visual-motor training a panacea for all the ills of childhood. If your boy or girl has a correctable medical defect, faulty vision or hearing, or a fairly deep psychological disturbance, this problem should be handled not by a teacher or parent, but by an expert practitioner in medicine, optometry or psychology. Remember that Jim, the boy in Chapter 1, was thoroughly examined by such experts and was declared "normal" before perceptual training began. (Remember also, however, that Jim's was a fairly typical case; that about four children in every ten have visual skills below the level required for good schoolwork; and that educational methods applied to teaching these skills hold out significant promise for each child so handicapped.)

Finally, be aware in using these techniques that you are functioning educationally rather than therapeutically—as a teacher, rather than a doctor or psychologist. This awareness will tend to keep your own attitude cheerful and patient, thus making the techniques we have presented here more fun for you and the child, and therefore more effective. As any good teacher will tell you, nothing is more interesting than a child, and nothing is more fun than teaching a child.

chapter 13 questions and answers

Question

If your emphasis on the importance of physical activities and motor skills is correct, then it should follow that professional athletes would be highly intelligent individuals. However, it is proverbial that these athletes are frequently inadequate in academic areas. How can this discrepancy be explained?

Answer

Knowledge and ability to perform basic movement patterns is fundamental to further development. However, as we have pointed out, higher skills are built upon these more elementary motor patterns. The possession of good gross motor patterns does not presuppose the development of the higher skills which are normally built upon them. Thus, in the hierarchy from motor skills to sensory-motor matching, to form perception, to symbolism, to verbal expression, to concept, the individual may drop out at any of these levels. Therefore, it is quite possible to have a highly developed motor pattern but to have failed to progress to the more advanced stages.

In the case of professional athletes, we have a highly selected group of individuals. The selection is made solely on the basis of motor performance. Therefore we would expect, as we find, a greater proportion of individuals who have stopped somewhere in the process beyond the motor stage than we would anticipate in the population as a whole. It should also be pointed out that not all professional athletes fit the popular picture. It is probable that as a group their academic ability is considerably higher than popularly supposed.

Question

Are programs of sports in the early elementary school ages good in the light of principles of development?

Answer

Most sports require a high degree of motor skill for successful performance. In a great many sports a variety of types of motor skills are required and the individual must be well versed in basic motor patterns in order to succeed. However, this is not always the case. Thus we have seen many children who are retarded in development and whose retardation begins with the basic motor skills. These children are frequently good in sports. But they pick their position and their function in the game with great care. In football such

115

a child will usually be found in the line, where all he has to do is sight on his opponent and lunge forward, using whatever modification of the walking pattern he may have available. In baseball he is usually the pitcher. Here again, he need only sight on the target and throw the ball. Very seldom is he found in the outfield where he has to alter his motor pattern on the basis of the direction in which the ball is coming. He frequently shows much less interest in basketball and, if he is interested, usually chooses a guard position where alertness and rapid modification of movement patterns is at a minimum. The sports program can offer excellent learning opportunities in the motor area. However, in order to benefit from these opportunities, the child must not be allowed to select and maintain a limited type of participation.

The sports program is highly oriented toward competition and team efforts. Through this we attempt to develop sportsmanship, co-operation, ability to get along with teammates, etc. All of these goals are admirable and we would not attempt to detract from their value. Nevertheless, from the developmental point of view the emphasis on competition results in the selection of the children who can perform motor tasks for inclusion on the team. The child who can't perform such tasks is not chosen and his experience with the motor aspects of the sports activity becomes very limited. From the point of view of the individual child, of course, this emphasis is exactly reversed. The child who can already perform is not in need, from the point of view

116

of his development, of additional participation. The child who can't perform, on the other hand, desperately needs more participation. This latter child, however, is the one who receives least. It would therefore be desirable if our concern with sports became more balanced. We should put relatively less emphasis on competitive and social aspects of sports and relatively more emphasis on developmental aspects. We should give relatively less attention to the child who can perform well for the purpose of making him a superior performer and give relatively more attention to the child who can't perform at all, so that we can bring him up to the level where he can perform to a minimum acceptable degree.

Question

My child rides a tricycle very well. He enjoys it and during his waking hours is very seldom off of his tricycle. He is highly skillful in maneuvering and has little difficulty in using it. Does this insure that he has adequate concepts of laterality and directionality?

Answer

We are concerned here with a single motor skill or a limited group of motor skills. Very frequently we find the child with an inadequate motor foundation who develops a high degree of ability in a limited skill. Since he can perform in this limited task adequately, he tends to channel all of his motor activity in this direction. He therefore develops a "splinter" skill. He shows an activity which is not related to the totality of basic motor skills but has been developed for itself

117

alone. As he continues to engage in this activity, the skill becomes further and further removed from total motor performance and is more and more obviously "splintered." Thus an unusual skill and interest in a specific activity such as riding a tricycle may not indicate adequate development of basic motor concepts such as laterality and directionality. In fact, it may indicate just the opposite: an escape from the problems of laterality and directionality through overconcentration on a limited area of performance.

Question

My child is too active. I cannot keep him quiet. He is always running about and is into everything. Does this overabundance of motor activity insure that he is developing the basic motor foundation for skills of a higher order?

Answer

In the case of most children who are described as "too active," it will often be found that their motor activity is spotty and unco-ordinated. The movements which they perform do not develop out of the total movement patterns of the organism but are a series of isolated movements of isolated muscle groups.

Many of these children show activity which can be described as "disorganized" or "disconnected." Such activities are probably the product of an inadequate general motor foundation. They represent the specific responses of the child which are all the responses he can make in the absence of a total motor pattern. Watch carefully to see whether or not his motor responses reflect the operation of the total organism or whether they reflect only the operation of specific parts or limited motor patterns. The motor activity from which the child learns and develops is activity of the total organism. It is co-ordinated and integrated. It is related to the welfare of the organism as a whole. Such children are usually not "overactive." Their activity is restrained and purposeful. It is engaged in for the purpose of co-ordinating total movement patterns.

Question

Shall I try to develop high degrees of skill in as many motor performances as possible in order to further the development of my child?

Answer

No. From the developmental point of view, the optimum condition is *not* high degrees of skill. *It is minimum ability in a wide number of motor activities.* As we have seen, behavior is based directly or indirectly on the operation of movement patterns. This does not imply that high degrees of skill are necessary. In any motor performance there is a minimum degree of ability which permits the child to perform the activity. This is the degree of ability which is important for his future development. Above and beyond this minimum degree of ability, highly refined and highly developed skills may be imposed. These skills may be desirable for certain specific purposes, but their contribution to general development is minimal. The law of diminishing returns sets in after the child has learned to perform the task adequately. *From the point of view*

119

of development, the acquisition of spectacular degrees of skill is not worth the effort required.

Question

I myself as a parent find considerable difficulty in performing some of the tasks which you have set for young children. Particularly the balancing and similar motor tasks give me difficulty. Does this mean that I do not have an adequate motor foundation for my behavior?

Answer

Remember that you are an adult. You have been through many experiences. These experiences have modified and altered your movement patterns. The stresses and strains of everyday living which you have endured have warped your motor performance. Therefore some of the things which should come easily to a young child come with great difficulty to you.

However, also remember that once upon a time you were a child. During your childhood you probably were able to perform these activities with ease. You developed these abilities and used them for the purpose of organizing the world about you. All of these early experiences left their traces in memory. Now, as an adult, you can call upon these memory traces to influence your behavior even though the actual motor activities may be very difficult for you at this age. Once an activity has been acquired, it is never completely lost and continues to influence behavior. We as adults are behaving daily on the basis of movement patterns which we are no longer able to perform. We are using memory images of past experiences to influence behavior. For this reason the problem with adults is quite different from the problem with children. The problem with the child is to teach him basic activities that find their place in memory and influence future behavior.

Question

What if the child fails to learn these basic skills and reaches the elementary or high school level before their lack is discovered? Is there anything we can do to make up this early failure?

Answer

We frequently find exactly the problem which you described among "retarded" children. We find children in the elementary grades and even higher who are not achieving adequately, and upon examination we find that they lack the basic readiness skills which we have been discussing in this volume. Experimentation and clinical work have both shown that it is possible in most cases to make up at least a major portion of the basic learnings which they missed. In order to accomplish this, we must go back to these basic readiness skills and teach them to the child just as we would teach them to a normal preschool child. Very frequently, in the case of the older child, the progress is more rapid. As we fill in the gaps he takes the necessary information and integrates it with additional information which, because of his age, he has been able to acquire. Thus he may pass through the various stages of training more rapidly than does the younger

121

child. We teach him, however, in exactly the same way and we insure that all of the stages of development we have been discussing are solidly laid, even though his age level would indicate that such skills are "beneath" him.

We have seen many cases in which children, retarded both academically and mentally, have been greatly aided by such a program. They have become noticeably more adequate and more able to adjust to their environment after the basic skills which they had missed were supplied.

Question

Is it possible to overemphasize basic motor skills?

Answer

Of course it is possible to overemphasize basic motor skills. It is possible to overemphasize any area of development. Development is a co-ordinated progress through various stages. Overemphasis can be placed on any one of the stages and will result in characteristic anomalies of development.

One of the most obvious relationships today is that between performance skills and verbal skills. Many of our current intelligence tests measure each of these two areas independently. Adequate development requires that both of these areas proceed together. At no point in development must we overemphasize one to the neglect of the other.

Our modern civilization, with its emphasis on automatic machines which do most of the manipulation for us, has become a highly verbal civilization. This development has been reflected in the sorts of experience which we present to our children. We present them with more and more verbal and symbolic material and less and less concrete and motor material. This discrepancy is particularly true among the higher socio-economic groups. It must be remembered that verbal ability can be no better than the fundamental motor ability which goes along with it. On the other hand, we cannot emphasize these basic motor activities to the exclusion of verbal experience. We must present the child with verbal activities and allow him to have verbal experiences along with his developing motor patterns.

Question

The games and activities which you have been discussing are not new. These are things we have done before. They have been described in books of children's games and books of activities designed for children. Why have the developmental advantages which you describe not accrued from the use of these activities previously?

Answer

It is quite correct that the activities which we describe are not new. They have been used for long periods of time. However, they have been used primarily as *single activities*. The goal of the activity was to develop the child's skill in the performance of this particular task. They were not used for the purpose of permitting the child to gain basic knowledge and basic abilities. The individual tasks were not related to the development of the child as a whole.

The important item in our discussion in this volume is the relationship between certain activities and certain basic knowledges and performances in the general behavior of the child. We are using specific activities not for themselves alone, but for the purpose of teaching some more basic and fundamental skills. This is the primary difference between the present suggestions and previous ones. *We are not here using activities for themselves alone, but for what they will teach.* No activity is considered independently but is considered as a contributing factor to some basic ability which the child requires in his development.

For this reason, it is extremely important to make clear that the activities presented in this volume cannot be used in a "cookbook" fashion. Merely putting the child through this series of activities will do nothing. It is not what we do, but why we do it that counts. In like manner, it must be remembered that the activities described here are certainly not the only activities which would be effective in teaching the basic skills in which we are interested. Other activities may be just as effective and in certain children more effective. Therefore the parent must first become well acquainted with the stages in development and know what it is he is trying to teach. Then he must select—either from the activities presented or from other activities gained from other sources, or from his own ingenuity—tasks which can be presented to the child and which will result in his learning the particular skill in which one is interested at the time. We must always approach the tasks from the point of view of the development of the child, never from the point of view of the task itself.

When we approach this series of tasks or any other series of tasks with the fundamental stages of development in mind, the tasks and the activities of the child in performing them take on an entirely new light. The activities engaged in and the learnings resulting from the activities become entirely different.

Question

We often hear the comment from public school personnel, "Let *us* teach the child." Frequently the public schools criticize parents for teaching children to read, etc. What relationship has this attitude on the part of the public schools to the type of program you recommend?

Answer

As we have pointed out earlier, the program which we have described here is a program of so-called readiness training. The object is to give the child the basic skills and abilities he will need to profit from the specific experiences which will be presented to him by the school system. With the exception of the emphasis on readiness in the kindergarten year, *this readiness program is primarily the responsibility of the parent.* As we have pointed out, the school assumes the *existence* of these skills when the child comes to them. The school will then be concerned with the *use* of these skills to gain certain knowledges and attitudes which will be

125

presented by the school curriculum. The school does not object and, in fact, encourages the parent to use every possible method of developing the readiness skills.

On the other hand, the teaching of academic subjects is a technical problem. Methods have been devised through experimentation and use in classrooms by which academic information can be most easily and most rapidly imparted to children. The methods which are used in the school system in your city may or may not coincide with the kinds of methods which were used when you went to school. The probabilities are that there will be rather marked differences. If the parent begins to teach the child academic material, he can only use those methods which were used when he went to school, unless he studies the whole field of education for himself. The result in most cases is that the child goes to school, having been taught some academic material by one method and now being taught the same academic material by a different method. The child is confused between the two methods of teaching and needless difficulties arise. Therefore, the school is quite correct in suggesting that parents do not teach academic material, but leave this to the school system. In this way confusion between methods of teaching will be minimized.

In some cases the child will acquire the readiness skills so readily and so easily that he himself desires to move on to more academic pursuits. Some children almost learn to read in spite of anything we do or fail to do for them. Some parents, therefore, will find their child "demanding" academic skills before he has reached the age where he can be enrolled in the public schools. Such parents should consult with the teacher in their community. She will be very glad to outline the methods used in the early stages of education and help the parents meet the needs of their child.

Question

If a child comes to school without the basic readiness skills, is there anything the school can do to help him in acquiring these skills?

Answer

The development of such readiness skills has become the primary concern of a number of kindergarten programs in this country. The kindergarten is attempting to supply whatever skills may have been missed by the child. The kindergarten is attempting in these cases to teach fundamental readiness skills. This program has proved very successful, and kindergartens have been performing an important function in insuring readiness for the curriculum of the early elementary grades. Children who have had kindergarten experience are found to have less difficulty in the elementary grades than children who have not had such experience.

If the child has not had kindergarten experience available, or if even this additional help has not given him the basic skills which he requires, something can still be done in the elementary school classrooms. Experimentation in the public schools of Lafayette, Indiana, for example, has shown that many of the activities which we have been discussing can be taught in the regular school classroom. Methods have been designed whereby these activities can be adapted to the classroom situation and the teacher can devote a certain amount of time to teaching readiness skills to those children who need it, without disrupting the classroom routine. These experiments have proved highly successful and have indicated that time spent in such readiness activities is more than made up by the future progress of the child in the academic curriculum.

Question

Is nursery school education desirable?

Answer

Nursery school education, where it is available, is highly desirable. The nursery school attempts to intensify, both quantitatively and qualitatively, the types of activity which will further the development of readiness skills in the children. These activities are intensified qualitatively by the technical knowledge of the nursery school teacher which makes it possible for her to present more specifically designed activities than are possible for most parents. They are also intensified quantitatively since the nursery school can present a wider variety of experiences than is possible in the usual home situation.

It must be borne in mind that nursery schools vary in quality. The value of the nursery school education to the child is directly proportional to the skill and background of the nursery school teacher. Therefore nursery schools must be selected with some care and attention must be given to the technical qualifications of the personnel.

It must also be remembered that *the nursery school does not supplant the parent.* The fact that the child is enrolled in a nursery school and is receiving nursery school experiences does not relieve the parent of his responsibilities as a parent in teaching and furthering readiness skills. The parent must evaluate the status of his own child and must accept the responsibility for seeing to it that this individual child's development is aided to the maximum degree. We cannot, as parents, shift our responsibility to the nursery school.

Question

How can I teach my child such fundamental concepts as honesty? Specifically, what can I do about his continual lying?

Answer

Lying in children is a very complicated behavior and can result from numerous causes. Many standard volumes on child development will outline for you the emotional and social problems in lying. Here we would like to discuss one additional factor which is frequently overlooked.

When the child lacks the fundamental readiness skills about which we have been speaking, he sees things and experiences things differently from children who have these fundamental abilities. It therefore follows that in any given experience what the child gets from this experience is somewhat different from what you get from it. In particular, the child's experience is frequently fragmentary. Only a certain part of the occurrence makes an impression on him. When he is asked to behave in terms of this experience, he frequently behaves in terms of this single item.

He overlooks all other considerations in the occurrence because, for him, *they did not occur*. When he discusses or tells about or behaves in terms of the experience, his behavior will be different from what we would predict on the basis of what we saw in this incident. We, as adults, however, compare his final behavior with our impression of the incident. To us, it looks as though he were lying, as though he were deliberately distorting the facts. As a matter of fact, there was not a deliberate distortion of fact but a distortion *in the experience of the fact*. Although it looks like it on the surface, the child is only telling us what he experienced.

The only basic cure for this type of lying is to supply the fundamental skills which will allow the child to experience the same thing from this incident that we experienced. We must help him by showing him the distortion in his experience and helping him to fill in the missing parts so that his experience will coincide with ours.

Question

How can I teach my child fundamental social relationships? In particular, how can I teach my child how to get along with his brothers and sisters?

Answer

Here again, social adjustment is a very complicated

problem and standard volumes are available which discuss in detail the emotional and social problems involved.

There is, however, a factor in social adjustment which has only recently begun to assume importance in our thinking. Many modern books speak about "social perception." Although this term has undergone a great deal of confusion, it means, basically, that two people cannot agree unless they see the same incident in the same way. This problem of social perception, therefore, brings us to the same considerations that we discussed above in terms of the problem of lying. Before two people can behave in a concerted fashion, they must see the situation in the same way and must experience the incident in the same way.

We overcome this difficulty primarily on the basis of the concept of averages. It is highly probable that no two people ever see the same situation in exactly the same way. One person will emphasize certain elements and de-emphasize others. The other person will have a different collection of emphases. The result is that no two people ever have identical perceptions of a given situation. However, as a result of our intercommunication with each other, we tend to strike an average between all of these different perceptions. We modify our perception in terms of what the next individual tells us about his; in like manner, he modifies his perception in terms of what we tell him about ours. As a result, these perceptions tend to gravitate toward an average. Here, as in the case of lying, the degree to which and the ease with which our perceptions approximate the average is dependent upon the amount of distortion which was present originally and the amount of experience we have had with other people whereby we can learn how to adjust to an average.

Many children have difficulty getting along with other people because their perceptions of situations are so distorted that they cannot see the same thing that the other person is seeing or experience the same thing that the other person is experiencing. There is, therefore, no common ground for agreement. The solution to such a problem lies in two directions. On the one hand, we must help the child to develop his perceptions so that what he sees and what he experiences will not be highly distorted. On the other hand, we must present him with the opportunity to learn through vicarious experience what other people are seeing and what other people are experiencing so that he will know what the average is. We must help him by supplying the fundamental skills which will permit him to experience adequately. We must help him by pointing out the differences between his experience and our experience. And we must help him by permitting him a wide range of contact with other individuals so that the average at which he arrives will be based on as broad a sampling as possible. It is only as individuals experience the same incident in a sufficiently similar way that they can behave toward that incident enough alike to permit an adjustment of the social relationships between them.

glossary

DIRECTIONALITY

Awareness of left, right—front, back—up, down—etc., in the world around you. This awareness stems from the internal sense of direction developed earlier, known as "laterality" (see below).

EGOCENTRIC LOCALIZATION

The earliest form of space awareness, in which the position of any person or object is defined in relation to oneself —"You are close to me; that chair is far from me." The next step is "objective localization" (see below).

GLOBULAR FORM

Over-all perception of an object without viewing its details and without understanding how the object is put together. This type of perception precedes the more complete and accurate "integrated form" (see below).

133

INTEGRATED FORM

Detailed and accurate perception of an object, including awareness of how the parts of the object go together to make a complete whole.

KINESTHETIC

"The knowledge of the muscles"—the sense or perception gained from the feelings created by one's own movements and bodily tensions.

LATERALITY

Awareness of left and right, etc., within one's own body; also, differentiating between one's left side and one's right side. Laterality develops earlier than "directionality" (above) and serves as its underpinning.

OBJECTIVE LOCALIZATION

Positioning objects in space in relation to one another— "The book is on the desk." "He is standing behind her."

PERCEPTUAL SKILLS

Techniques of seeing and understanding, most of which are learned rather than innate, and can therefore be taught.

PERCEPTUAL TRAINING

The process of educating people, most particularly children, in learning to see things accurately, rapidly and completely.

POSTURE

A dynamic, shifting control of one's body, which to be "good" should be loose, flexible and comfortable.

PSYCHOMOTOR SKILLS

Techniques of controlling the movements of one's body. These skills are partially self-developing and partially learned. As a result, they can be taught.

Glossary

READING READINESS

Preparedness to learn to read, based upon the previous learning of numerous psychomotor, postural and perceptual skills.

VISION

Seeing in the sense of understanding. "Good vision" is a function of smooth and precise working relationships between the eyes and the mind.

Drawing toys
pegboard Game
Marsden ball on string ⟩ teach child skills necessary to reading

index

Index